NATURALISTIC FLOWERS

NATURALISTIC FLOWERS
A Year of Plants, Places and People

AESME STUDIO

With over 270 illustrations

CONTENTS

6   Preface by Jess Lister
12   Introduction by Ally Lister

20   **THE PINK HOUSE**
Trinity Cottage, Aldeburgh, England
October

32   **WINTERING IN THE WEALD**
Sissinghurst Castle Garden, Kent, England
November to March

46   **WOODSMOKE & JACARANDA**
Lake Naivasha, Kenya, East Africa
November to December

66   **EPHEMERAL FORMS**
St Ives, Cornwall, England
April

88   **AN INTERWOVEN HOUSE & GARDEN**
Turn End, Haddenham, England
April

98   **THE SILVER ORCHARD**
Les Terres de Pierre, Provence, France
May

112   **AN IRREVERENT IDYLL**
Great Dixter, East Sussex, England
July

130   **STILL LIFE**
Charleston Farmhouse, East Sussex, England
July

146   **HINTERLAND**
North Norfolk Coast, England
July

168   **FOOD & FLOWERS**
Edinburgh, Scotland
August

188   **I BLIXEN-STILEN**
Rungstedlund, Rungsted, Denmark
August

202   **SOLACE IN NATURE**
Serge Hill, Hertfordshire, England
September

216   **THE WILD WEST**
Aberglasney, Camarthenshire
& Dyffryn Fernant, Pembrokeshire, Wales
October

234   Directory
235   Acknowledgments
236   Authors' Biography
237   Index

Preface
Jess Lister

We're often asked how we manage to work together as sisters. The truth is, very happily. This book is the expression of a shared passion and love of working side by side.

Al introduced me to the world of flowers. Through them I discovered gardening, spending the last ten years creating a cutting garden to supply the studio with materials. With no prior experience and a blank canvas of grass and brambles, it has been a decade of intense work. Our half-acre plot is a place of supply, and of learning. What varieties can we grow, how do they change through the seasons, will they last when cut? If we leave these seeds to self sow, or choose not to stake or prune, how will the materials change?

By her own admission, my sister has an insatiable appetite for designing with flowers. She's unafraid to experiment; the wilder and weirder, the better. To allow for limitless creations, the garden houses a vast range of colours and textures throughout the seasons, layers of bulbs, annuals and perennials nurtured through organic practices; it serves as both a source of inspiration and a biodiverse habitat. This naturalistic approach translates directly into the vase. Arrangements have an immediacy and a sense of spontaneity, conceived as they are from walking among the beds, looking closely at what is flowering at that precise moment in the year. Seasonal restrictions pay dividends in the pure joy of harvesting the 'first' of each species: bunches of fresh sweet peas, unfurling rose buds, tiny wild strawberries. There is beauty to be found in senescence too, and no material is overlooked, whether windswept, weedy, diseased or past its prime.

PAGE 2
A meditation on the detail, shape and intricacy of individual stems.

PREVIOUS
An alleyway of hollyhocks (*Alcea*) in North Norfolk.

OPPOSITE
Jess in the Nuttery at Sissinghurst Castle with a clutch of Balkan anemones (*Anemone blanda*).

Gardening flows naturally into my other role: making films about flowers. It's not uncommon, I think, to have spent much of my early urban adulthood suffering from a case of 'plant blindness', unaware of the extraordinary flora in my everyday existence. Now, with a camera in hand, I use my eyes in a different way – seeking out nuances of colour as the light changes, spying the movement of insect legs on the underside of a leaf. These tiny yet cinematic moments are what I love to bring to life on screen for our viewers.

Previously ambivalent to seasonal change, I've learned that November (my birthday month, incidentally, and one I used to associate with the onset of bad weather and darkening afternoons) is in fact my favourite time to be outside, filming the garden in its finale of crackling colours, rosehips and glowing grasses illuminated in the setting sun.

Photography allows for a change of pace from filmmaking. Shooting this book gave me a chance to look deeper, further and more closely than ever before. Each chapter represents a time of total immersion in a special place – whether for a couple of days or just a few hours – and a chance to appreciate being in the moment, savouring the finer details, together.

RIGHT
Midsummer at our Hampshire cutting garden.

OPPOSITE
A spontaneously gathered bouquet of garden flowers, weeds, grasses and fruits.

OVERLEAF LEFT
Field poppy (*Papaver rhoeas* 'Amazing Grey'): petals the consistency of crushed silk, with colours that shift from stormy blue to slate and pearl with the occasional red bleed.

OVERLEAF RIGHT
Garden to vase: a fan-shaped arrangement in a footed terracotta vessel in The Hovel at Great Dixter.

Introduction
Ally Lister

When you arrange flowers all else fades away. The mind stills, the body calms, the world grows quiet. Mental chatter and anxieties recede into insignificance. What remains is an awareness of the present moment. Sidelight coming through the open window, the gestures of your hands, the water in the vase, the interplay of wood, leaves, petals and the shadows they make on the wall. Flowers are beautiful, of course. They have an aesthetic power that can instantly change the atmosphere in a room and bring it to life – an effective, if short-lived form of decoration. But more than this, arranging flowers speaks to some ancient part of us that yearns for a connection with nature and each other, seeming to belong to another time.

Playing an instrument, moulding clay, painting a landscape – these are all things that allow us to escape our everyday concerns and our fast-paced, increasingly online existence. Having arranged flowers for over ten years now, I know that this unique blend of nature and art is more beneficial and relevant than ever. It is a true craft, a particular skill honed through practice, concentration and discipline, enlivened and enriched by curiosity and a willingness to experiment. What elevates a flower arrangement beyond the technically accomplished or just superficially pretty is spontaneity and individual instinct. What these years – and countless arrangements – have slowly revealed to me, is that the pleasure of arranging flowers is to be found in the process, the making, rather than simply the finished composition.

Plants; Places; People. We return to this simple three-word mantra time and again. Plants – because the materials are paramount and we are, more than ever, in love with using local, seasonal ingredients. Places – because climate, landscape and weather are intrinsic to what

LEFT
Dawn in East Africa. Ally gathers fennel (*Foeniculum vulgare*) and African rosemallow (*Hibiscus acetosella*) from an organic market garden on the shores of Lake Naivasha.

those materials will be, and because an arrangement will look most beautiful when in harmony with its background. People – perhaps this really comes first and foremost. Our flower films are watched by people all over the world. Created to inform, inspire and entertain, for many these films also offer a calming escape from the stresses of everyday life. Through our workshops, we have had the privilege of bringing people together from ten to eighty years of age, watching them make flower arrangements and witnessing the joy this brings. By sharing the love of this practice with others, you realize that the crux of it all is a celebration of being alive and in the moment. Without people, there would be no creativity, no conversation, no vases, no gardens, no written word and no one to enjoy flowers with. With this, the ancient part of ourselves yearning for a connection with nature and with each other, is satisfied. What a very rare and precious thing.

Naturalistic flower arranging is intended to celebrate the materials we are lucky enough to harvest and to display them in a way that evokes the way they grow in the soil. A light touch is needed to draw out each flower's unique characteristics and behaviours. As in naturalistic garden design, we are mimicking nature – choosing materials that 'look right' together because they share the same season, climate

RIGHT
A Japanese kenzan, which we use in place of floral foam.

OPPOSITE
Naturalistic arranging is a style and philosophy that aims to evoke the way flowers naturally grow and behave on the mother plant.

or growing conditions. We champion overlooked materials like weeds and celebrate the full life cycle of plants, returning green waste to the garden to be composted and to nourish the soil for future flowers. As such, we choose not to use floral foam (which doesn't biodegrade), instead favouring the use of Japanese kenzans and re-usable chicken wire for support in the vase.

This philosophy steers away from the rigidity of traditional floristry, bypassing restrictive rules and formulas in favour of taking simple cues from the plants themselves or the environment in which they have been growing. It requires a degree of restraint. Rather than contorting stems and flowers, the ingredients are, to a certain extent, allowed to dictate their course and given space to shine. Materials are of primary importance, so we will happily go above and beyond to ensure they are freshly harvested and in season. This ethos is prevalent in the 'slow food' movement, where it is acknowledged that a locally and organically grown tomato, roughly chopped, drizzled with good olive oil and a little sea salt can't be bettered. One perfect peach for pudding. It's the same with flowers. If you have interesting ingredients, arranging them need not be mathematical or overly laboured (and this goes for designing for large events as much as arranging flowers at home). We believe in learning through doing and that experimentation and practice are key to developing our craft. There is always more to learn.

Finding flowers specifically for each project has always been an integral part of our work process. When we first started the studio (and the garden was still in development) we'd source from a range of places and mix them all together: foraged blackberry briars with hydrangea from the market; marigolds from a local kitchen garden; a neighbour giving away dahlias. Part of the magic was the conversations we would have and the snippets of information gleaned – how the weather had affected the lengths and shapes of the stems, recommended varieties and conditioning tips. The garden is now home to (too) many beautiful plants, but it's fair to say the excitement of finding new materials to arrange with hasn't diminished.

Writing and photographing this book, and travelling away from the studio and garden, we re-discovered the joy of hunting for materials. In each place I made spontaneous arrangements from what I could gather around me, with very little prior planning and often limited time, while Jess sought out interesting plants, weaving together the spirit of each place through a series of photographs. Along the way we spent time with the most extraordinary flora and fauna – gathering aloe vera overlooked by colobus monkeys (Woodsmoke & Jacaranda), sailing through swathes of sea-lavender in the Norfolk salt marshes (Hinterland), filling vases in settings steeped in gardening history (Beauty & Freedom) and finding connections between flowers and art, food and therapy. We have sought out interesting colours, shapes and textures everywhere from pavement cracks and hanging baskets to rocky mountain paths, filling our notebooks with stories from talented growers, gardeners and farmers keen to share their passion for flowers.

We will never forget this year, the elation of creating freely and the collaborative sense of intimacy that comes from working together as sisters. I hope we've managed to capture a feeling of joyful discovery in these pages, and that, in sharing our adventures, you may find floral inspiration, allowing us to introduce you to some very special plants, places and people along the way.

OPPOSITE
The joy of arranging with unfamiliar materials, learning from the organic form, shape, colour and texture of each ingredient.

THE PINK HOUSE
Trinity Cottage, Aldeburgh, England
October

The season changes in increments, almost imperceptible unless you're paying attention. Shadows grow heavy, the light is green-gold. Glittering spiders' webs are strung across the garden. For flower growers, October is the beginning of a new year – even more so than January. With the start of the autumn term, another gardening year commences, and our thoughts turn to preparing in earnest for spring. Ahead of plunging into the next chapter in the garden, we decide to get on the road for a few days in search of rest and creative inspiration. Where to? Somewhere within an easy drive of London. Somewhere coastal, to blow the cobwebs away. Somewhere to recharge low batteries and to nurture the seed of an idea in our minds. We stick a pin in the map. Suffolk.

We're staying in the small coastal town of Aldeburgh. Trinity Cottage is a peachy-pink corner terrace on the main street. Minutes from the seafront, it's the country retreat of our friend Kristin Perers, a photographer. After a wet summer and warm autumn, the leaves on the trees are only just beginning to turn. The landscape has that warm, golden tint of autumn on it, the halcyon, gently shifting reeds stretch as far as the eye can see.

This is Benjamin Britten country. On the banks of the Alde his eponymous concert hall rises like a ship out of the marshes. The river is tidal, narrowing north-west to meet the Ore and eventually emptying into the North Sea. The first afternoon we follow the sailor's path into the marshes; blue smoke from a smouldering bonfire drifts in mid-air. Away from restless toddlers, we enjoy an undisturbed night's sleep and wake before dawn to watch the sun rise on Dunwich Heath. It is chilly, the first cold spell of the autumn, so we pull on layers, shivering.

PREVIOUS
Daybreak on Dunwich Heath as autumn descends.

LEFT
High water in the River Alde as it carves its way through the reed beds of *Phragmites australis*. This common reed (or Norfolk reed) has been used for thousands of years in thatching roofs. The long stems bear grey-green leaves and dusky, pinkish brown panicles of flowers.

The sun begins to rise above the watery horizon as we reach the cliff path, casting a thin beam of light across the sea and onto the headland. The heath is carpeted with bronze bracken and scratchy heather with the last tiny purple bells clinging to their wiry stems. Every so often there is a patch of bright yellow gorse. It is said to be haunted, this stretch of the coast, the thriving port town lost to the sea in the thirteenth century following a surge of storms. According to locals, when the wind is up you can hear the bells of lost churches ringing from beneath the waves.

Fortified by sea air and the beauty of the natural scenery we sit by the fire as night falls, drinking sour cherry tea, skin stinging from the afternoon's seaspray. The wind whips down King Street and the slim, wizard-y fingernail of a moon hangs in the sky. We turn over the seed of our idea for this book. A year arranging seasonal flowers in different places. How interesting and freeing it would be to create spontaneous arrangements with no preconceptions of how the end result would turn out, experimenting, being in the moment. Using new materials, learning about the plants growing in each place. We fall asleep to the sound of a storm brewing, waves crashing onto the beach, the taste of cherries mingling with the brackish water still on our lips.

RIGHT
Bracken (*Pteridium aquilinum*).

OPPOSITE
Arriving in the small seaside town of Aldeburgh, meaning old (Alde) fort (burgh). Once a Tudor port and a thriving centre for ship building, the town was granted borough status by Henry VIII.

OVERLEAF LEFT
Aldeburgh to London, 94 miles.

OVERLEAF RIGHT
The glittering pollen dust of roadside *Cyclamen*.

FINDING FLOWERS
Genius loci

A great deal of the joy of flower arranging is in the choosing and refining of materials. Selecting a vase. Gathering the ingredients. Whether foraging, cutting from the garden or sourcing from a farm or supplier – it's the thrill of the hunt. This process of combining the forms of flowers and foliage, as well as colours and textures, is always exciting because each time there is the opportunity to learn something new. Everywhere we go we see plants, both familiar and unfamiliar. In every space, both cultivated and wild, there is potential. At Kristin's kitchen table we put this theory to the test.

We've brought a couple of buckets of flowers from our Hampshire garden, the last of the season. Over a cup of tea I make some simple arrangements with roses and chrysanthemum, adding in a couple of stems of radiant pink *Cyclamen* (✿) picked up yesterday at an honesty box plant stall on the outskirts of town.

But what I am more drawn to, here, is the novelty of the maritime plants we've encountered the last couple of days on our coastal walks – the paper lacework of yellowing bracken on Dunwich Heath (*Pteridium aquiline*), the common reeds that grow all around the Maltings (*Phragmites australis*), the weeds and wild grasses (✿) along the strip of land that hugs the coastline.

On Aldeburgh beach, with slanting rainstorms in the distance, we find the yellow-horned sea poppy (*Glaucium flavum*) (✷), which grows wild only on the seashore, never inland. The bright flowers are gone now, leaving only the silvery, scalloped leaves nestled in the shingle. There is red valerian or 'kiss-me-quick' (*Valeriana rubra*) and common mallow (*Malva sylvestris*), a straggling perennial with streaked rose-purple flowers. Further along we discover common fennel (*Foeniculum vulgare*) (✷), which proliferates wild along the verges, introduced by the Romans for medicinal and culinary use. Considered an invasive species in Australia and the United States, here it loves the dry, poor soil of the coast. We pick a few stems and hold them up against the liminal margin between sky and sea – a flattering grey-blue backdrop.

Fennel, Reed, Valerian

Common fennel (*Foeniculum vulgare*)
Common mallow (*Malva sylvestris*)
Common reed (*Phragmites australis*)
Red valerian (*Valeriana rubra*)

Bowl by Chloe Rosetta Bell
Kenzan

OPPOSITE
A simple arrangement of four ingredients that grow wild along the Suffolk coast.

I arrange the foraged wildflowers in a small ceramic bowl with a pearlescent grey glaze. Picked from the immediate surroundings they seem more able and eager to evoke the distinctive atmosphere and spirit of this place, a little Suffolk town on the North Sea coast.

For a naturalistic effect the dusty pink reeds are positioned as they naturally grow, tall and upright. The mallow leaves and crimson-flowered valerian mingle together in a low scribble, since this is how they appear on the shingle beach. The common fennel has feathery leaves, slightly faded with the end of the season, a sharp, aniseed-y scent and hollow stalks – pleasing to cut. I snip the leaves from the fennel, adding a few of the nebulous wisps of foliage and umbels, and discard the stalks.

In his epic poem *Theogony*, Greek poet Hesiod described Prometheus stealing the ember of fire from the gods to give to mankind. He stole a red-hot coal from Mount Olympus and hid it inside a woody fennel stalk. For defying him and allying with mortals, the mighty Zeus condemned Prometheus to eternal torment – bound to a rock, each day an eagle would eat his liver and each night it would grow back, only for the same agony to be repeated day after day.

WINTERING IN THE WEALD
Sissinghurst Castle Garden, Kent, England
November to March

As we move towards winter we embark on a collaboration with Sissinghurst Castle Garden that will take the form of a botanical installation spanning the winter months. Our brief is to come up with four designs, sited at the entrance and underneath the Elizabethan tower, to celebrate materials from the garden and reflect a spirit of place as autumn turns to winter and winter to spring.

Deep in the folds of the Kentish Weald, Sissinghurst is one of the most beloved historic gardens in England. It was created by Vita Sackville-West, who lived and gardened here from 1930 until her death in 1962, and her husband Harold Nicolson. Vita's gardening style was characterized by ruthlessness when it came to change and improvement, and meticulous planning with regard to colour, shape, texture and seasonal planting, balanced with a love of the naturalistic and dishevelled. She allowed wildflowers to invade the garden (within reason) and plants that had self-seeded to take root where they fell. This was a place where beauty ruled. 'If roses stray over a path, the visitor must duck', wrote her daughter-in-law Philippa Nicolson. Now owned by the National Trust, the garden has been under the stewardship of head gardener Troy Scott-Smith since 2013. His goal has been to retain the unique character of the garden that Vita and Harold created while not remaining frozen in time – to move it on and to keep experimenting.

More than any other garden I know, Sissinghurst is suffused with an atmosphere of sensuality and heady romanticism. Ancient, lavish and yet intensely private in feeling (despite the hundreds of daily visitors), the exuberance of the planting ensures that you are wrapped in beauty from the moment you step across the threshold.

PREVIOUS
The first of an evolving, four-part botanical installation at Sissinghurst Castle Garden. Antique cast-iron urns overflow with rambling roses and their colourful hips.

LEFT
Windblown dahlias and Japanese anemones create a dishevelled sense of romance in the Rose Garden, all the more poignant as the season changes.

The White Garden is Vita's most renowned creation. Stunning in its apparent simplicity, it also exemplifies the collaborative nature of her relationship with Harold. Her artistic vision was made possible by his structural, architectural ordering – a 'succession of intimacies' as he called them. The white blooms and silvery foliage are contrasted against the geometric cruciform parterre of clipped box and the enclosing yew hedging. For me the real magic is in the orchard, where garden meets wilderness. It comes alive in spring with shadowy pools of *Narcissi* and wood anemones beneath the crab apples, and is glorious later in the summer when roses scramble up through their gnarled boughs and winding paths meander through tousled grass. And then there is the Nuttery – an avenue of Kentish cobnuts that, from late February, is carpeted with crocuses, melting later into *Scilla*, occasional spires of *Euphorbia*, the nodding bells of snake's head fritillary (*Fritillaria meleagris)* and drifts of primroses (*Primula vulgaris*). It is like walking through a painting.

RIGHT
December reflections in the Moat at Sissinghurst.

OPPOSITE
Bottles of early spring delicacies under the entrance arch.

FINDING FLOWERS
Senescence and Renewal

In the November gloaming the garden shrugs on a low mist at dawn and dusk. An avenue of winter-flowering cherry trees (*Prunus* × *subhirtella* 'Autumnalis') (✸) in the Rose Garden is scheduled to be felled due to disease. We choose one to use for height and structural substance in the first phase of the installation. The leaves are mottled, raspberry pink, apricot and lime, adding a flickering flame effect to the entrance arch as the nights draw in (✿). The garden team are busy pruning roses. We amass large bundles of European hornbeam (*Carpinus betulus*) and exquisite arching rose canes smothered with hips (✿), strands of gleaming porcelain berry vine (*Ampelopsis glandulosa*) (✸) and branches of Cornelian cherry (*Cornus mas*) (✿). By early December, winter has begun in earnest. The silhouettes of deciduous trees are almost leafless and the Nuttery is a cathedral of arched cloisters, a complex lacework of fine stems. It is now that you can see the beauty of the garden's bare bones, the definable structure of each room and skeletal forms of seedheads still standing. In the beds chocolatey soil and bronze leaf litter is offset with flashes of yellow gold and rust, pools of icy white and the silver-grey of glaucous leaves. Here and there gleaming berries and rosehips add touches of vibrant colour, the last roses clinging to naked stems like shreds of ragged silk. Twisted *Clematis* offcuts and apple branches smothered with lichen provide the starting point for a vast, swirling Christmas wreath, woven with layers of glossy evergreen foliage – box (*Buxus sempervirens*), yew (*Taxus baccata*), bay (*Laurus nobilis*) and beckoning English holly (*Ilex aquifolium*). A thin iron arch is dressed with greenery, rosehips and a gold-to-silver garland of dried flowers. Spiralling up through the foliage these ingredients have a glittery, metallic quality – masterwort (*Astrantia*), honesty (*Lunaria annua*) and sea kale (*Crambe maritima*).

> 'Consider too *Crocus Tomasianus*, small,
> so pale, Lavender cups of tiny crockery'
> *The Garden*, Vita Sackville-West

In the New Year there are remnants of snow on the ground. The gardens are flowerless, at their barest before the first bulbs emerge, and our installations focus on dried materials stockpiled from the previous year (✤). The painstaking pruning of roses and trees is ongoing; in the Nuttery the garden team are coppicing hazel and dividing Barrenwort (*Epimedium*) beneath. Chartruese (*Carpinus betulus*) catkins and yellowing leaves provide a cheerful hit of colour. By February, the hours of daylight are at last lengthening and the gardens are awash with colourful spring bulbs. Lilac crocuses (*Crocus tommasinianus*) (✱) – as well as mustard (*Crocus chrysanthus* var. *fuscotinctus*), ice-blue white squill (*Scilla mischtschenkoana*) and spring starflowers (*Ipheion uniflorum*) are soon joined by primroses (*Primula vulgaris*), Lenten roses (*Helleborus* × *hybridus*) (✤) and whorled fritillary (*Fritillaria verticillata*) (✤). The sight of hundreds of tiny, jewel-like flowers sets our hearts racing. Jess, so engrossed in her photography, is at one point lying flat on the freezing stone path, anything to be nose-to-nose with crocuses shivering in the breeze. On the outskirts of the garden we find a fallen oak tree. The skein of sinuous limbs proves a useful, sculptural way to enclose pockets of spring bulbs from the nursery, planted in a mix of bokashi compost and bark (✱).

My final arrangement is a simple, rustic display using the last bundle of cherry (✤). Felled four months ago, this tree has been the backbone of our installation at every stage, and several branches are still in full bloom. The timing and the sheer beauty of these flowers seems to signify so completely the miraculous regeneration of the natural world – loss and hope and renewal, the dying with the emergence of new life. Another season of flowers on the horizon at last.

Rosehip, Chrysanthemum, Great Mullein

Chrysanthemum 'Allouise Orange'
Chrysanthemum 'Avignon Pink'
Cornelian cherry (*Cornus mas*)
Great mullein (*Verbascum thapsus*)
Stinking iris (*Iris foetidissima*)
Rosa 'Blush Rambler'
Rosa 'Multiflora'
Rosa 'Wickwar'

Cast iron urn
Liner bucket
Chicken wire

Roses are synonymous with Sissinghurst; Vita loved their lavish generosity and planted possibly over three hundred varieties. Much to Harold's chagrin, she pruned only lightly, leaving the unruly mass of stems for nesting birds. In the orchard, we pilfer bundles of rambling rose prunings from the gardeners for their slender canes, elegant leaves and fiery hips.

A footed garden urn of iron, decorated with *Acanthus* leaves, to welcome visitors as they enter through the weathered wooden gates. The crumbling brickwork offers a mosaic backdrop of cream, terracotta and rust with a pitted biscuit texture and I pick out both paler and brighter shades for the arrangement, allowing the rose stems to cascade and drape in a languid way. (If you are a gardener you might see this as more of a ravening scramble). The silver-grey mullein spires provide a vertical form, leading the eye upwards. A sparing sprinkle of *Chrysanthemum* - the last flowers of the season - meet the outstretched arm of a *Prunus* branch and the slow, pleasurable fade from flaming orange through tints of copper, maroon, apple green, lemon and lime. Looking out across the first quad your attention snags on a flash of gold beneath Vita's writing tower and from there the smouldering autumn garden awaits.

PREVIOUS
Christmas at Sissinghurst – evergreens, metallic seedheads and a garland of rich, dusky velvet and silk at the entrance to Vita's writing tower.

LEFT
Welcoming guests to the garden with a sculptural display of autumnal branches, entangled with the spindling whips of rambling roses studded with hips in a collection of antique garden urns – an open-armed invitation to step inside and experience the garden at this precise moment in the year.

WOODSMOKE & JACARANDA
Lake Naivasha, Kenya, East Africa
November to December

We arrive at Jomo Kenyatta airport in Nairobi late on a Friday night and the familiar, smoky scent of the city receives us. It is over a decade since we have been back to Kenya; in our twenties, we made regular trips and fell in love with the beauty of the landscape – the light before dusk, which is blue but also golden, a welcome respite from the brittlest of the English winter months.

In the morning we open the crittall door, stepping out onto rich red soil and into an orchestra of birdsong. It has rained overnight, a sponge-springy mat of clover and grasses soaks the hems of our pyjamas, steam rising into the air. We walk the perimeter of the garden, inspecting the plants: *Agapanthus, Aloe, Thunbergia, Jacaranda*. Vibrant and exotic they are so very different to our sleeping winter garden back home.

We spend the day running errands around the leafy suburb of Karen, driving down roads lined with *Bougainvillea* – Schiaparelli pink, white, tomato red, lilac, orange and apricot. Everywhere there are familiar names, sounds and smells: Ngong, Mbagathi, Dagoretti, the honking and screeching of traffic, the perfume of frangipani blossoms mingling with exhaust fumes and the drifting scent of charred meat from the shops selling *nyama choma* (roasted goat). Langata Road is

PREVIOUS
Vibrant rills of organically grown vegetables as the sun rises on a November morning in Kenya.

LEFT
Papery *Bougainvillea* petals on the garden path in Karen, Nairobi.

flanked with plant stalls, rows upon rows of colourful flowers, shrubs and trees lined up in the red dust. It's nearly Christmas; gaudy red-ribboned wreaths glitter on gates and jubilant high school graduates are swathed in tinsel garlands. Just before dusk we walk softly around the house where the Danish writer Karen Blixen lived from 1917 to 1931, marvelling at the yellow bell orchid tree (*Bauhinia tomentosa*) in the darkling garden, its pale lemon flowers glowing against the misty blue outline of the Ngong Hills.

The next morning, car piled high with luggage and essentials, vases nestled gingerly between, we head north on the Nairobi-Nakuru Highway towards Naivasha.

RIGHT
A rustic ceramic vase, decorated with zebras and *Acacia* trees, from the Opportunity Factory in Nairobi.

OPPOSITE
Garden flowers from the shore of Lake Naivasha including *Salvia*, *Papyrus* and *Bougainvillea*.

FINDING FLOWERS
Sarah's Salvia

'I'm afraid I've very little in flower now except the *Salvia*', Sarah says as she walks us around just before twilight. We're on the lawn of her home on the south side of Lake Naivasha searching for flowers to arrange. In the distance the lights of the town glimmer across the water and on the western shore a ghostly grove of *Acacia* (✺) skeletons rise out of the water, the trees drowned by the rising lake. In the branches above our heads, monkeys quarrel and play. Sarah is a knowledgeable and capable plantswoman and gardening here is not without its challenges – from buffalos and baboons to long periods of drought and an infestation of Lubber grasshoppers that decimated her beloved *Aloes* and succulents. The tree with the pink blossom dangling beneath the verandah is *Prunus cerasoides* 'Puddum' (✺), she tells us with a giggle – a wild Himalayan cherry native to southern and eastern Asia. We're immediately drawn to a sweetly scented weeping vine clinging to the garden wall. Jasmine? No – sandpaper vine (*Petrea volubilis*) (✺).

The garden, built in the form of staggered terraces and lawns, overlooks a panoramic view of the lake. It's open to the game sanctuary beyond, the fences removed and a watering hole installed to encourage the wildlife in – zebras, giraffes, impalas and warthogs. There is no obvious boundary around the garden itself – at some indiscernible point it just melts into the bush and down the slope to the papyrus grove on the shore of the lake, where hippos grunt between drifts of floating water hyacinth (*Pontederia crassipes*). Scattering a flock of helmeted guinea fowl we discover the bright pool of *Salvia* – white, lilac and red, a hedge of *Bougainvillea* (✺) opposite a grove of frangipani trees, the waxy white blossoms falling onto the grass with a soft thud.

Pulling on my tallest boots, I fill a bucket with a little water and, hoping very much that I don't meet one of the resident pythons, cautiously inch deeper into the garden beds. Cutting here feels so different to an English garden – tropical and potentially dangerous. From the still black water of the (decidedly snake-y looking) terrace pool grows dwarf papyrus (*Cyperus prolifern* 'Cleopatra') echoing in miniature the larger forms of *Cyperus papyrus* on the shore of the lake below. I brave it, reaching in for a few stems. So far so good. Next – a few succulent *Aloe vera* next to African starbush (*Grewia occidentalis*) (✺) – avoiding the serrated 'teeth' along the edges of their leaves and admiring the tall, stiff stalks with spikes of tubular coral flowers.

During our stay we meet Sarah's friend Diana, whose family run a small-scale commercial flower farm a few kilometres away. After a visit to the farm one morning, we sit on the verandah enjoying the sunbirds and a slightly different view of the lake. In Diana's garden are countless varieties of kaleidoscopic *Bougainvillea*, geranium to deter snakes, *Salvia*, orange, guava and grapefruit. She kindly allows us to snip a few branches of the lilac, tangerine and coral *Bougainvillea* to take back with us. We choose a few of the long thorny canes and reverently wedge them in the boot of the Landcruiser. 'It probably won't last', she warns. As it turns out, she is right.

Prunus, Plumbago

African starbush (*Grewia occidentalis*)

Blue jacaranda (*Jacaranda mimosifolia*)

Cape leadwort (*Plumbago auriculata*)

Himalayan cherry (*Prunus cerasoides* 'Puddum')

Footed ceramic vase from the Opportunity Factory, Nairobi

Chicken wire

In Nairobi we were lucky to find a footed ceramic vase, decorated by hand with paintings of zebra and Acacia trees. Sarah gifts us a few gnarly branches of the Himalayan cherry. Part of the fun of garden-to-vase arranging is having an idea for a colour palette but not quite knowing what you are looking for until you find it. In this case, the sky blue stars of *Plumbago* blended with the cherry to create a pleasingly pretty concoction.

The vase isn't watertight, so inside goes a re-purposed ice cream tub and a ball of chicken wire for scaffolding. I choose branches that will help to create a sculptural, leafy composition. First the *Prunus cerasoides*. In India this is regarded as a sacred or holy tree, the leaves often combined with wild citrus fruits to create wreaths for decorating alters during the Hindu festival of Maha Shivaratri. *Jacaranda* is an ornamental tree imported from the Americas, which thrives in the warm Kenyan climate. In November it is the end of their flowering season here. The ferny leaves and violet, bell-shaped flowers are a delight. I add the vibrant blue *Plumbago* last, liberally dotting their whippy stems through the other branches at varying heights. *Auriculata* means 'with ears', referring to the shape of the leaves.

PREVIOUS
Early morning sunlight glancing off *mabati* roofs in Sarah's garden on Lake Naivasha.

OPPOSITE
A light, frothy arrangement of flowering branches for the side table in a peaceful bedroom.

African starbush (*Grewia occidentalis*) is an evergreen shrub native to south-eastern Africa with dark-green leaves and star-shaped flowers; it is difficult to propagate and likes best to pass through the gut of a monkey before germinating.

Jammy Mouth & Barbados Gooseberry

Barbados gooseberry (*Pereskia aculeata*)
Blood sage (*Salvia coccinea*)
Bower of beauty (*Pandorea jasminoides*)
Jammy mouth (*Ruttya fruticosa*)
Natal grass (*Melinis repens*)
Paper flower (*Bougainvillea* – varieties unknown)
Queen's wreath (*Protrea volubilis* 'Albiflora')

Sisal basket from Hadithi Crafts
Kenzan
Chicken wire

OPPOSITE
Containers made of woven natural materials like sisal, willow or reed make interesting vases for flower arrangements; they just need a watertight liner – a jar, bucket or repurposed food packaging will all suffice. We save a lot of ice cream tubs and yoghurt pots!

OVERLEAF LEFT
Slenderleaf rattlepod (*Crotalaria ochroleuca*), a leafy vegetable native to Africa and grown by many indigenous tribes who value its high yield, tolerance to disease and poor soil and usefulness in medicinal applications.

OVERLEAF RIGHT
Jess photographing at dawn among the cabbages at Ecoscapes.

In Nairobi we buy a group of woven baskets. These have been made from the *Agave sisalana* plant by a collective of female weavers in the Kasigau region of south-eastern Kenya. Basket weaving is a traditional craft in Taita culture. The collective is called Hadithi, which means 'story' in Swahili.

I select a ginger-coloured basket to arrange in, finding a place in the entrance hall where the light is flattering against a pale-yellow wall. The basket isn't watertight, so inside I slip a plastic jar with a kenzan (flower pin-holder) in the base, capped with a small dome of chicken wire. I start with a few stems of Barbados gooseberry or lemon vine (*Pereskia aculeata*), letting one long scrambling stem tumble down the front. The leaves are waxy and a delicious cocktail of apricot, mustard and lime. I add a couple of branches of the amusingly named East African 'jammy mouth' (*Ruttya fruticosa*). Then three surviving stems of Diana's *Bougainvillea* and sprays of the intricate bright white Queen's Wreath. While we are working, there is the soft thud and scuttle of Colobus monkeys landing on the *mabati* roof. The bright red tropical sage (*Salvia coccinea*) are dotted through next, then wisps of smoky pink *Melinis repens*, a perennial grass native to Southern Africa – this bunch gifted to us by Diana. And lastly a few trails of bower vine (*Pandorea jasminoides*), which usefully softens the base of the arrangement, its lilac blooms hanging downwards like tropical bells or flowers from back at the beginning of the world.

FINDING FLOWERS
A Farm in Africa

The next stop of our trip is Ecoscapes, an organic market garden just over the headland, perched on the edge of Korongo Bay on the western shore of Lake Naivasha. It's a uniquely beautiful sight to see the seams of multi-coloured vegetables, neatly tended by the farm workers in their chore coats and wellingtons, with giraffes and waterbucks grazing beyond the perimeter. The crops are planted in multiple small plots and then repeated in evenly spaced grids; there are streaks of rhubarb, sweet potato, horseradish, corn and Savoy cabbage (✸), rows of citrus and pomegranate trees (*Punica granatum*) (✣). Some we recognize because we grow them at home – borage, artichoke, lentil, courgette. Others are unfamiliar – Daikon or mooli, the cucumber-tasting African thorn melon, okra and turmeric.

Ecoscapes is the project of Alex Bell, a landscape designer and plantswoman. Here, in the heart of the Great Rift Valley, she grows over a hundred different varieties of vegetables, fruits, herbs and flowers for home delivery locally and in Nairobi. On the farm there is also a plant nursery, specializing in native perennial plants. A small herd of Jersey cows produces milk, butter, mozzarella and ricotta, the rich manure helping to fertilize the farm crops. The garden occupies around twenty of the private hundred-and-twenty-acre wildlife sanctuary, the abundant crops criss-crossed by red dirt tracks.

When we arrive at the farm the short rains would normally be coming to an end but this year they are forecast to continue until February. Shadowy thickets of *Acacia* trees are strung with lush overgrowth. Swathes of creeping African horned cucumber (*Zehneria scabra*) are punctuated with bright blue African lily (*Agapanthus*) (✣), the curious, harsh calls of ibis birds echoing between them. Among the outlining grass verges there are flowers we wouldn't be surprised to see growing wild at home: hemp agrimony (*Eupatorium cannabinum*) or in cottage gardens – orange tassel flower (*Emilia coccinea*), *Verbena* and society garlic (*Tulbaghia violacea*) (✸). More exotically there is arrowroot (*Maranta arundinacea*), bright yellow country mallow (*Abutilon mauritianum*), the sweet-looking but foul-smelling lilac puffs of billygoat weed (*Ageratum conyzoides*) and tiny daisy-like blackjack flower (*Bidens pilosa*), which we arrange informally in a trio of sisal baskets (✣). I'm excited to discover the exquisite *Cleome gynandra*, (✣), commonly known as saget, cat's whiskers or most poetically spiderwisp. The stems are interestingly curved, interspersed with dangling pods, the flowers a soft grey-white. We've seen *Cleome* grown as a cut flower at home; this variety is native to the tropics and subtropics of Africa. The seeds, shoots and leaves are edible and nutritious with a bitter, mustard-like flavour and anti-inflammatory properties; rich in folic acid, it is used in African communities by pregnant and breastfeeding women.

Hibiscus with Lemon

Cranberry hibiscus (*Hibiscus acetosella*)
Fennel (*Foeniculum vulgare*)
Great millet (*Sorghum*)
Lemon
Marigold (*Tagetes patula* 'Bonita')
Natal grass (*Melinis repens*)

Footed ceramic vase from the Opportunity Factory, Nairobi
Chicken wire

One morning Jess and I rise at dawn and zig-zag our way across the fields, calling out to one another in excitement every so often across the beds. We cut materials efficiently, before the sun is hot on the back of our heads, carrying sloshing buckets on our hips back to the cottage where we're staying. On the back porch we quickly condition the stems, stripping the dross foliage and hastily tucking them back into cool water to rehydrate. We return to the buckets later with rapidly diminishing daylight in which to do them justice; dusk falls on the Equator as softly and swiftly as a snuffed candle. Cicadas chorus in the grass, there is the sweet smell of burning charcoal in the afternoon air. A farm cat purrs on the bench, until, nap interrupted, she lazily rises to catch a beetle crossing the porch.

It is autumn at home – perhaps I'm still craving turning leaves as I select the materials for a distinctly fruity colour palette of dusty red and mustard, every ingredient similarly colour-shifting and nuanced. The starting point is the cranberry hibiscus, otherwise known as African rosemallow and some feathery fennel. It needs a dash of something stronger – a clutch of marigolds sprinkled throughout. The citrus is too exciting to pass up. For texture and a glinting metallic addition, I add millet. Last but not least, the rose natal grass (*Melinis repens*) given to us by Diana – an inflorescence of silky pink fluff, like candy floss.

LEFT
In place of a branch, I use tall stems of great millet for height. To the left, a casually arranged bunch of marigolds in a blown glass goblet with strawberry swirls by Kitengela Glass.

Great millet (*Sorghum*) is a grass domesticated from its wild ancestor more than five-thousand years ago in what is today Sudan.

EPHEMERAL FORMS
St Ives, Cornwall, England
April

Paddington to Penzance: hours of green blurred through a train window. It is early spring but has been unseasonably warm for weeks. Lavished with water, the countryside is verdant and plush with new growth, flooded in many places, and when the sun breaks through the cloud cover, which it does only rarely, the plants are eager to bloom. Gardens are already awash with lilac and the woods with carpets of bluebells. We have packed cameras and raincoats and a few flowers from our garden. They are bunched, carefully wrapped in brown paper and encased in a tall wheelie trolley, meadowsweets (*Spiraea*) and ninebark (*Physocarpus* 'Summer Wine') protruding from the top. We get some odd looks on the train.

On the last leg of the journey we snake through Carbis Bay, where artist and sculptor Barbara Hepworth lived in the 1940s with her painter husband Ben Nicholson and their triplets, before moving to the studio in St Ives where she would spend the rest of her life. The headland is flecked with gorse (*Ulex europaeus*) and alexanders (*Smyrnium olusatrum*), the sea an arresting silt-less turquoise. By next morning a new weather front has rolled in overnight, drenching the town with a fine white mist. We climb the steep, cobbled hill to Trewyn Studios early. The streets in the old town are narrow, labyrinthine and still quiet. The studio is essentially a one-up one-down, two large rooms over two floors. To the rear, a walled garden wraps around outhouses that became Hepworth's carving workshop and yard, and a lean-to greenhouse where she grew *Pelargonium*, cacti and jasmine. 'Finding Trewyn Studio was a sort of magic', wrote Hepworth. 'For ten years I had passed by with my shopping bags not knowing what lay behind the twenty-foot wall... Here was a studio, a yard and garden

PREVIOUS
Considering balance and form with the exquisite *Fritillaria* 'Green Dreams' in the Cornish studio of the late Dame Barbara Hepworth.

LEFT
Hepworth's 'Two Forms (Divided Circle)', 1969, with *Prunus* 'Accolade', a deciduous cherry with bright, lime green leaves and semi-double light pink flowers in spring.

BELOW
Bound for Penzance (left), St Ives harbour (right).

RIGHT
Camellia japonica beside a bronze cast of Barbara Hepworth's hand viewed through 'Pierced Form (Epidauros)', 1960.

where I could work in open air and space.' We're working today in the studio – on the first floor, which is now a gallery. This upper floor was Hepworth's wood-carving and painting space from 1949 and the next year, following her separation from Nicholson, it became her bedroom and living room. I am later told that the exact spot where we chose to set up – on a white gallery plinth beside the window – was where Hepworth's bed was, and where she died in 1975 in a fire.

You bring flowers into a room and they change the energy and dynamic of the space instantly and entirely. We have been dreaming of arranging flowers here for a long time and it seems a little surreal now to be looking at an empty vase on a gallery plinth between Hepworth's sculptures with the bells of St Ia's chiming in the town below. How uncanny to be working in the space of someone you admire but who is long gone, listening to the same church bells toll that they must have listened to innumerable times, witnessing the same slant of light from the high windows illuminating your tools and materials.

There is a physical rhythm to arranging flowers that is like a dance. Twisting, spiralling, leaning, reaching. Repetition, in practice, is essential for improvement. We can use the same flowers and revisit the same outline shapes over and over – but each time we create something unique. Whenever we use a new vase we are exploring the specific interplay between that vessel and the flowers. And each time the result is something that will never be exactly repeated.

Barbara Hepworth musingly drew comparisons between sculpture and dance. So too did her friend Bernard Leach – known today as the 'father of British studio pottery' – whose workshop we visit the same afternoon, just a mile inland. 'A practiced hand who makes the same shape over and over again, eliminates all unnecessary movement, and the result and speed is, to the person who sees it for the first time, something of a miracle. But so it is with all good handcraft, and that repetition is extremely important, in the history of craftsmanship. It's like repetition in dance, for example. One might think it would be boring – tiring, always doing the same thing, but it's not always quite the same thing, and the dance isn't.'

Bernard Leach (1887–1979) discovered pottery-making on a trip to Japan in 1911. 'I was carried away to a new world. Enthralled, I was on the spot seized with the desire to take up the craft.' He trained as

OPPOSITE
A bottle vase by Britta James with a Chün glaze containing slender branches of Japanese spirea (*Spiraea japonica*) with the wild tulip (*Tulipa* 'Sylvestris') and locally foraged alexanders (*Smyrnium olusatrum*).

ABOVE LEFT
A kick-wheel in the throwing room at the Leach Pottery acts as Ally's 'lazy Susan'.

ABOVE RIGHT
The kiln at Leach Pottery, loaded for firing.

an apprentice two days a week for two years under Urano Shigekichi, known as Kenzan VI, a descendant of the renowned 17th-century potter Ogata Kenzan. Returning to England in 1920 with his great friend Shōji Hamada, Leach built the first *noborigama* (a wood-burning climbing kiln) in the West in St. Ives and founded the Leach Pottery. They used locally felled wood and *Rhododendron* to fire the first kilns, and bracken to create wood ash glazes.

Leach described his work in bodily language, often referring to a vessel's lip, neck, belly or foot and the human quality of each piece, acknowledging its individual character, its strength, or quietness. Over the next fifty years he was responsible for elevating and celebrating the humble material of fired clay, advocating simple, utilitarian functionality in a style based on traditional Japanese, Chinese, Korean and English slipware. The pottery produced a range of hand-crafted Standard Ware for sale to the general public and Leach published many books, travelling widely as a lecturer. In 1966, he was awarded Order of the Sacred Treasure Second Class in Japan – the highest honour given to a non-national – and, in 1974, the equivalent of the Nobel Prize during his final visit to Japan.

From its humble origins as home and workplace, one hundred years later Leach Pottery has grown and evolved to encompass a busy working studio, education centre, museum, shop and gallery space. An active community of artist-potters in residence keep Leach's traditional values alive, championing functionality, honesty and the rich artistic exchange between East and West.

OPPOSITE
Pierced Form (*Epidauros*), 1960 by Barbara Hepworth with handheld Spanish bluebell (*Hyacinthoides hispanica*).

OVERLEAF LEFT
'Finding Trewyn Studio was a sort of magic', wrote Hepworth. She purchased the space in 1949; two years later, she divorced Ben Nicholson and it became her permanent home.

OVERLEAF RIGHT
Looking into Hepworth's working studio, with floral reflection. Her overalls are still hung along the back wall, as though at any minute she might return to her workstation.

FINDING FLOWERS
A Sculptor's Garden by the Sea

The Trewyn Studio garden is green and lush, its west Cornish setting and sub-tropical climate lend the space, enclosed within thick granite walls, the feeling of a Mediterranean courtyard. Hepworth's sculptures are interspersed throughout the plantings on white-painted breezeblock piles but the garden was a private working and relaxation space rather than an intended location for displaying her work. It is not possible to know how Hepworth perceived the garden design in relationship to the placement of the sculpture, or vice versa, and it is likely that she chose plants that appealed to her aesthetic preferences. She was a reasonably experienced gardener, having worked in a market garden and turned her own over to vegetables during the 'Dig for Victory' campaign in World War II. In 1949 she met and befriended the composer Priaulx Rainier who would regularly stay at Trewyn over the coming years. The two women shared a belief in the restorative effects of nature and the interaction of rhythm and form, and they greatly influenced and inspired one another's work. Rainier was very involved with the development of the garden studio and reconfiguring its layout and design.

This morning, in the rain, it is a steaming haven, a miniature jungle. We weave through and around the sculptures, beneath New Zealand cabbage palm (*Cordyline australis*). We brush past paperplants (*Fatsia japonica*), *Mahonia japonica* and New Zealand flax (*Phormium tenax*). A huge sixty-year-old bull bay (*Magnolia grandiflora*), planted by Hepworth, provides a canopy over the studio building. It is before the museum is open to visitors and we can feel the artist in the garden, not just because we are surrounded by her work, but in the contrasting forms and the juxtaposition of the plants - Spanish bluebell (*Hyacinthoides hispanica*) (✸), unfurling ferns, *Camellia japonica* (✿), the glade of shivering bamboo, *Phyllostachys nigra* f. *henonis*, encircling 'Conversation of Magic Stones', the architectural forms of arum lilies (*Zantedeschia aethiopica* 'Crowborough') and satin magenta flowers of giant herb robert (*Geranium maderense*) (✿), the largest of all geraniums.

Beneath the dense green overgrowth there are pools of bluebells, yellow primrose (*Primula vulgaris*) (✸), blue forget-me-nots and stinking hellebore (*Helleborus foetidus*) in the shade. You can hear the sound of the sea, and the cries of herring gulls. I recognize Chilean iris (*Libertia ixiodes*) (✿) - warmer here, it is further along than my potted one at home in London, and already flowering. Beyond the sheltering hedges of Japanese spindle (*Euonymus japonicus*) we can see the church tower and the staggered rooftops of the town, the graceful curve of the bay beyond under grey clouds like swirling ash picked out with green daubs of alexanders (*Smyrnium olusatrum*) (✿).

Green Dreams and Camellia

Bridal wreath (*Spiraea* × *vanhouttei*)
Coral bells (*Heuchera* 'Marmalade')
Crab apple (*Malus* 'Prairie Fire')
Crab apple-scented gum (*Eucalyptus stuartiana*)
Daffodil (*Narcissus* 'Actaea')
Japanese camellia (*Camellia japonica* – variety unknown but possibly 'Pompone')
Ninebark (*Physocarpus opulifolius* 'Summer Wine')
Persian buttercup (*Ranunculus* 'Elegance Rosso')
Persian buttercup (*Ranunculus* 'Picotee Pink')
Persian lily (*Fritillaria persica* 'Green Dreams')
Summer snowflake (*Leucojum aestivum*)
Tulip (*Tulipa* 'Foxtrot')
Tulip (*Tulipa* 'Pieter de Leur')

White ceramic vase, made in Kyoto
Chicken wire

'Pierced Form (Epidauros)', 1960. Barbara Hepworth

PREVIOUS
Every arrangement begins with looking closely at the shape, form, colour and texture of each ingredient.

LEFT
Exploring the relationship between positive and negative space. Sculpture, garden design and floral design all invite interaction and contemplation.

Camellia japonica from Hepworth's garden in a fluted ceramic vessel with an organic ribbed texture. An old favourite, we found this vase in Kyoto a few years ago; it is now well-travelled. Its curvature suits the light, white space and the sculptural shapes of the spring branches – bronze-leafed ninebark 'Summer Wine' and *Spiraea* × *vanhouttei* with fine green leaves.

I make a tall outline shape with the branches. Their curving stems make for an elegant asymmetric 'V'. *Eucalyptus stuartiana* fills in, its grey-green leaves speckled with plum. The *Malus*, with clusters of raspberry blossom and khaki-maroon foliage, and locally grown pink tulips contrast with the sylph-like *Fritillaria persica* 'Green Dreams'. These stems are suitably sculptural and seem happy to recline sideways to show off their pistachio bells.

I group the flowers dark to light with a ribbon of white *Narcissus* 'Actaea' and the precious *Camellia* clustered in a grouping of three – the odd number being visually pleasing for such an obvious 'focal'. Lastly, I add *Leucojum* as a gestural element to bring in some light curves, a few ruffly *Ranunculus* and *Heuchera* 'Marmalade'.

With the flowers beside them, the sculptures in the gallery seem to come to life, as though by a natural material they are woken from passivity by their proximity to living – and dying – forms. Later we move the arrangement around the room to see how it interacts with the sculptures and paintings. Through 'Pierced Form (Epidauros)', 1960, it is framed by a perfect sphere, after some patience to find the right angle. Beyond, the aged cherry tree – *Prunus* 'Accolade' – itself sculpted by the sea winds, is just beginning to flower, buds dripping with raindrops.

Snowflake, Bluebell, Periwinkle

Daffodil (*Narcissus* 'Sophie Girl')
Foam flower (*Tiarella cordifolia*)
Fringe cups (*Tellima grandiflora*)
Intermediate periwinkle
  (*Vinca difformis* 'Snowmound')
Naples garlic (*Allium neapolitanum* 'Cowanii')
Periwinkle (*Vinca major*)
Persian buttercup (*Ranunculus* 'Picotee Pink')
Pointed-petal fritillary (*Fritillaria acmopetala*)
Snake's head fritillary (*Fritillaria meleagris*)
Spanish bluebell (*Hyacinthoides hispanica*)
Summer snowflake (*Leucojum aestivum*)
Tulip (*Tulipa clusiana* 'Lady Jane')
Windflower (*Anemone coronaria* 'The Bride')

Ceramic beaker
Chicken wire

At the studio in London, we have a moodboard onto which we pin inspiration in the form of photographs, poems, letters, recipes and drawings. Among the evolving collage one postcard has survived for many years – a portrait of Barbara Hepworth in a beret and Breton sweater, flanked by arrangements of flowers in glass vases. The photograph was taken for a book, *Unit One: The Modern Movement in English Architecture, Painting and Sculpture*, published in 1934. Who made the flowers? Hepworth herself? Constance Spry, perhaps? It is clearly spring. Despite being a black-and-white photograph you can clearly make out the forms of *anemones* and *ranunculus*, although Hepworth is wearing sandals. A warm spring? Perhaps she just didn't mind getting cold feet for the sake of a good outfit.

In an interview in 1959 Hepworth said, 'Life will always insist on begetting life [...] This continuity contains a tremendous and impelling force. In autumn all the dynamics are laid for spring.' As I make the arrangement opposite, I think how vital and resilient the blues of spring are. Found everywhere in nature – in sea and sky – they are nevertheless somehow startling after the white-grey of an English winter. From here a loosely analogous colour palette forms – cool shades of white, blue, pink, purple and plum, and a proliferation of bell shapes – snakeshead and pointed-petal fritillaries, summer snowflakes and fringe cups, juxtaposed with the soft contours of *ranunculus* and *anemones*.

On the turntable outside Hepworth's workshop are blocks of marble still waiting to be carved. Tools are slung together on the workbench. Behind, the soft colours of her assistant's overalls as though they have just been hung up, dusty from a long day's work.

LEFT
Hepworth in the Mall Studio, London, 1933.

OPPOSITE
Spring forms – rosettes, bells, stars and umbels in a simple cylindrical jar, using an uncarved block of Hepworth's marble as a display plinth.

Chilean Iris in a Quiet Pot

Coral bells (*Heuchera* 'Marmalade')
Coral bells (*Heuchera* 'Mega Caramel')
Fairy wings (*Epimedium* × *warleyense* 'Orangekönigin')
Japanese spiraea (*Spiraea japonica* 'Autumn Princess')
New Zealand satin flower (*Libertia ixioides*)

Pot by Matthew Foster, The Leach Pottery
Kenzan

OPPOSITE
A small, humble arrangement of garden flowers in memory of Barbara Hepworth and Bernard Leach and the creative dialogue they shared.

As with any craft, the practical task of arranging flowers relies upon a collection of everyday tools and objects. My essential toolkit includes a pair of Japanese carbon-steel snips with a walnut handle, a curve-bladed pen knife (for the quick and efficient removal of thorns and splitting stems), a roll of coated chicken wire and a collection of kenzans (again, made in Japan). With these to hand, I feel empowered to work spontaneously and comfortably, wherever I am. Over the years I have developed an increasingly particular – and occasionally sentimental – attachment to these items. Refining what works and what doesn't is personal and dependent not only upon on aesthetic preference, but also our own physicality – the size of our hands, the weight of the tool, the way it feels to hold. A fundamental part of any flower arrangement is the vessel. Functionally this vase or container holds water to keep the materials alive for as long as possible but it is, by necessity, an integral part of the overall design. Our preference is for individual, hand-made ceramics – those that are attractive but unassuming and functional. I like vases that have a tactile quality, are stream-lined and simple but that have a unique personality to them, a character of their own.

Another indispensable part of my flower-arranging kit is a lazy Susan (this allows you to spin the vase as you go and to see the arrangement from all angles as it is made). In the hundred-year-old throwing room at The Leach Pottery, I'm delighted to find that one of the kick-wheels suitably fulfills this purpose. After a little practice, I get the hang of the gentle, meditative momentum of the wheel and slowly make a simple arrangement in a footed pot with a *tenmoku* glaze, described by its maker Matt Foster as a 'quiet pot'. Unpretentious and calm, it is a pleasure to handle and an ideal base for the fiery *Heuchera* leaves. I use these as a focal point in their own right; as beautiful as any flower, the foliage is ruffle-edged, a complex network of veins etched across a downy surface, deep raspberry underbelly beneath. For delicacy, filler and colour – *Spiraea* and fairy wings with tiny, spidery flowers. The pure white of the *Libertia* catches the light and appears to be in conversation with the rest of the arrangement.

AN INTERWOVEN HOUSE & GARDEN
Turn End, Haddenham, England
April

Some places pleasantly haunt you; Turn End is one such place. After my first visit some years ago it kept cropping up in my dreams afterwards, a persistent, beckoning intrigue, which was elusive in itself. Why do certain places capture our imagination? Perhaps it is the way they change with the light or time of day or the seasons, or they make us nostalgic for times and places from our past. We become the painter who returns to the same scene over and over, never quite feeling they have decoded whatever it is that makes up the specific atmosphere of a place.

Turn End is reclusive and personal, a sequence of secret spaces wrapped in curving roughcast walls at the heart of a Buckinghamshire village. It is a world-renowned example of how modern houses needn't resemble the averagely ugly, poorly planned suburban developments that have blighted many rural English villages and towns up and down the country. The L-shaped trio of contemporary living spaces has a beautifully stark and stripped-back simplicity, constructed during the 1960s using local, traditional building techniques and materials. The architect Peter Aldington still lives here with his wife Margaret (who once said 'I only came to terms with being a housewife because I built the house'), and it is his synchronous design of the buildings and garden that you step into from the entrance courtyard.

PREVIOUS
'No-man's land' and the pergola at Turn End in the Aylesbury Vale.

OPPOSITE
Archways in the wichert walls link a series of distinctly varied garden spaces.

I remember that first time, stepping around the bamboo screen. Where *are* you suddenly? Certainly rooted in the historic fabric of a small village in middle England – the distinctive wichert walls (indigenous to the Vale of Aylesbury) are richly textural, rendered in a corruption of white earth, local, lime-rich soil puddled with straw and pantiled above. And yet there is a strongly familiar flavour of Japan in the compact spaces that unfold like origami as you walk further in, the concrete, wood and glass, the almost reverential tranquillity of the Japanese temple garden in the bamboo and pine, the gravel, the detailing and dark wood, the rock garden a minute landscape of alpines. There is a Californian essence too, perhaps it is the long, low roofs clad in warm terracotta tiles and the intimate courtyards of varying sizes that lead one into the other, a twenty-one-metre-tall (69-ft) Giant sequoia (*Sequoiadendron giganteum*) rising above them.

RIGHT
The central axis of Daisy Court aligns with the wooden pergola and large ceramic urn by Svend Bayer on one side, the Coach House and Box Court on the other. It is an intimate but stunningly effective vista, with a profusion of planted pots.

OPPOSITE
Three houses and a garden: the entrance to Turn End is flanked by a happily planted *Deutzia* × *elegantissima* 'Rosealind'.

FINDING FLOWERS
Haddenham Specific

The delight of this half-acre garden, once the slither of an elderly orchard of apple and pear trees belonging to the village baker, is in the way it embraces the house, unravelling around large trees – chestnut, walnut, robinia and wattle – in a spool of compact spaces, each with its own character. For a relatively small plot, so many different – and contrasting – gardens are achieved within this space. There are courtyards, glades and pergolas, a Mediterranean 'no-man's land' with four square borders all higgledy-piggledy with plants, a woodland spring garden, and summer borders stuffed with sun-loving perennials.

You can sense as you walk the stone or gravel paths that this intimate, maze-like garden was created sculpturally, by hand, by someone with a hunger for plants and an instinctive way of putting them together, particularly in terms of scale and texture. The house and garden are one, they seem to constantly spill into one another. There are numerous sightlines, constant visual pulls created by open archways in the tactile wichert walls, enclosed courtyards, pergolas and cleverly placed stoneware urns. The sense of layout and scale is playful; the smallest space houses three of the largest plants – umbrella bamboo (*Fargesia murielae*) and roses 'Félicité et Perpétue' and 'Cécile Brünner'. There are swathes of naturalized planting. Plants have been allowed to self-seed and crop up in unexpected places throughout the garden. Poppies like crinkled tissue paper traverse the gravel, seeding happily into nooks and crannies.

It is April and the countryside is effervescent with cow parsley and marguerites, that rush of fresh energy as the earth warms and spring comes into view. Jackie Hunt (the gardener here for the past fourteen years) greets us warmly and we walk around together, stopping to inspect areas of particular floral interest. I tell her that the *Tradescantia* she gifted me from the greenhouse when I was last here in the autumn is slowly taking over my kitchen windowsill. Entering the intensively planted 'no-man's land' – in summer a riot of colour – we're led in a trance-like state through the adjoining garden rooms. There are some exquisite roses flowering – *Rosa moyesii* 'Hilleri' (✸) and *Rosa* × *odorata* 'Mutabilis' (✿), hot pink honeysuckle (*Lonicera hispidula*) (✿) and bearded iris (*Iris germanica*) (✸) as well as intriguing drifts of *Fritillaria* gone to seed (✿).

Walking through the garden we're reminded how design mediums can overlap and inspire one another. Art, architecture, garden design – there are many shared principles that can be applied on a smaller scale and overflow into flower work. Careful, considered design. Taking time to assess, practice and experiment. Using local, salvaged or recycled materials. Prioritizing natural light. Achieving a contemporary style with traditional methods. In all these ways Turn End has influenced our own garden and living spaces, and our arrangements too.

Rambling Rose and Rock Rose with Bearded Iris

Bearded iris (*Iris* × *germanica* 'Monsoon Moon', 'Smokey Dream', 'White City')

Deutzia × *elegantissima* 'Rosealind'

King's spear (*Asphodelene lutea*)

Rock rose (*Helianthemum* 'Henfield Brilliant')

Rosa 'Cécile Brünner'

Sicilian honey garlic (*Nectaroscordum siculum*)

Resin bowl

Kenzans

As a flower arranger you can become obsessed with a particular setting – an alcove, a mantelpiece, or, say, a concrete bench above a pool of water. I could envisage a flower arrangement here long before it became a reality – it's been hovering at the back of my mind for a few years. The sill cantilevered over the water, the shadows and reflections, the uneven stone path creeping through the courtyard, *robinia* leaning overhead, Noisette rose hugging the house. For this spring arrangement I wanted to evoke the quixotic nature of 'no-man's land' – groupings of fiery and cooler colours, a strong outline form juxtaposed with a wildly romantic sense of overflow.

I foot the ladder and Jackie cuts two curving canes of the sweetheart rose 'Cécile Brünner'. The choice of container is a low resin bowl with a collection of kenzans to near enough cover the base. I start with the roses, fixing the thin wiry stems onto the pins and allowing them to cascade down to the left-hand side, the tips of the leaves trailing in the water. On the opposite side I counter-whisker using the naturally arching stems of *Deutzia*, which has cupped pink flowers. The bearded iris have appropriately architectural forms and are positioned tall and upright, as they naturally grow, in an asymmetric staggered formation beginning with the olive-yellow 'Monsoon Moon' followed by bronze 'Smokey Dream' and 'White City' at the top, palest blue fading to white. The waxy bells of honey garlic are interspersed, also upright. For a few brighter pops of colour, I add the gold stars of King's spear and lipstick-red rock rose. This grows in a low, compact form and so I place them as filler or 'ground-cover' around the base of the iris.

OPPOSITE
A naturalistic arrangement allowing each variety to behave as they naturally do on the plant – the iris, allium and king's spear are tall and upright, the roses cascade and sprawl, the rock rose acts as a low filler or ground cover.

THE SILVER ORCHARD
Les Terres de Pierre, Provence, France
May

The 'Little Alps' – a place of arid limestone peaks and dry valleys. Nestled in the foothills, Les Terres de Pierre comprises twenty hectares of olive, fig and pistachio trees in a series of orchards interspersed by stony tracks, streams and pine trees. We stumbled across the farm of William and Prune Revoil by chance some years ago. Decorating a wedding with flowers just the other side of St-Rémy-de-Provence, we were searching for a house to rent that could accommodate the event preparations, extra floral helpers and our young families. The discovery was serendipitous and we quickly fell under the spell of the place with its particular atmosphere, crumbling stone walls and dusty olive groves.

    William and Prune moved here from Paris ten years ago with the intention of breathing new life into the property, which has been in William's family for several hundred years. Throwing himself wholeheartedly into the life of the farmer, first to create his own olive oil and latterly wine, Prune left her job working for Chanel *haute couture* and established her own atelier (she specializes in *plummasserie*, the intricate art of featherwork) and together they renovated and decorated the L-shaped farmhouse. At the heart of this is the cavernous kitchen where William prepares delicious meals using local produce and copious amounts of his golden olive oil.

PREVIOUS
Wild oats (*Avena fatua*) blowing in the wind at dusk.

OPPOSITE
Evening among the olives.

We arrive towards the end of May. It is a mild spring with a pleasantly cool wind, much greener than our previous visit when the land was crisp and yellow following a period of drought, and William correspondingly glum about the effects this would have on his harvest. The wildflowers here are delightful and beyond counting. Days assume an unhurried routine. Buying bread, pastries and vegetables from the village. A daily loop of the olive groves, always enthusiastically chaperoned by Doundoun the English Setter whose white, long-legged form slinks ahead into the trees. Occasionally Maurice the cat walks a little way before stopping to languidly clean a paw, watching after us with his green eyes. In the afternoons we stay close to the cool of the house, sitting in the shade of the almond tree, reading in the hammock as our children play in the gravel *pétanque* pitch or collect fallen figs.

RIGHT
Field poppies (*Papaver rhoeas*) grow wild throughout the farm.

OPPOSITE
Ally picking wildflowers accompanied by Doundoun the English Setter.

FINDING FLOWERS
Foraging in the Olive Groves

It is late spring and not yet hot. There is a watery quality to the light. The olive groves have a silvery coolness. Beneath them are pooling carpets of textural grasses and wildflowers, picked out in painterly daubs of stronger colours. Our circular walks are scented with thyme and rosemary and warm rocks. We notice different plants depending on the light and the hour – at dusk, the sunbleached oats (*Avena fatua*) glow in a ghostly sea of rustling bracts. One evening we spot a wild boar snuffling around under the pine trees. We stop and stare but he only flicks us a cursory glance and trots away into the shadows. Alongside the stream we find sharp rush (*Juncus acutus*), tiny wild wood pinks (*Dianthus sylvestris*), sweetly scented hedge bedstraw (*Galium mollugo*) a scrambling sticky perennial weed misted with white stars, vibrant broom (*Spartium junceum*) and woolly bindweed (*Convolvulus languginosus*) – short-stemmed, with pink funnel-shaped flowers. Beneath the olives are clusters of lilac-blue field scabious (*Knautia arvensis*) (✱), shrubby hare's ear (*Bupleurum fruticosum*) and common mallow (*Malva sylvestris*) (❁) encrusted with minute white snails. Here and there, field poppies (*Papaver rhoeas*) and love-in-a-mist (*Nigella damascena*) (✿) thrive in the disturbed soil. In this Mediterranean climate and rocky setting, the plants are tough yet have a deceptively fragile quality.

Flower arrangements drift together slowly, the materials gathered in a sporadic fashion, a few stems here and there as we find them. Morning-time is accompanied by the bubbling of stovetop coffee, nectar-sweet apricot juice in the afternoon, or an ice-cold glass of rosé as the light begins to fade. The garden wraps the house in scent and the fizzing sounds of busy insects among the honeysuckle (*Lonicera periclymenum*) (✱), lemon verbena (*Aloysia citrodora*) and lemon balm (*Melissa officinalis*) (❁). At the back door an oleander (*Nerium oleander*) smells faintly of almonds. A mat of blue rock bindweed (*Convolvulus sabatius*) (✿) creeps over the step onto the *terrasse*. The honeyed stone of the old farm buildings lend a soft and tactile backdrop to arrangements. Here earthy containers seem a fitting choice – terracotta pots that have been hand made locally for centuries.

On our last afternoon, Prune carries a heavy antique flower press down to the front porch from her studio. We select the best examples of each variety and layer them between sheets of translucent paper. She tightens the metal plates and says with a shrug that she will let us know how they turn out. A few weeks later I receive a voice message and some photos of the framed artwork, like a cross section of the landscape between crisp black card and glimmering glass, wafer-thin flowers and grasses and leaves, all perfectly preserved.

Seeded Apple with Seedpods

Asparagus fern (*Asparagus setaceus*)
Pomegranate (*Punica granatum*)
Scabious (*Scabiosa stellata* 'Sternkugel')

Stone bowl with foot
Kenzan

PREVIOUS
Arranging on a sultry afternoon, keeping company with Maurice the cat.

OPPOSITE
An arrangement of high tonal and textural contrast: the scratchy asparagus offsets the pitted stone backdrop and diaphanous seedheads.

At the adjoining corner of the 18th-century farmhouse is an arched stone passage and, to one side of the shuttered wooden doors at the far end, an alcove with a low stone shelf. The honey of the stone and soft grey of the plaster wall behind is a flattering setting for an arrangement. The large sculptural dish was a starting point for a more contemporary design using just three massed ingredients. Just through the doors the garden beyond is flanked by compact fruiting shrubs and the pomegranate is in flower. A stream carves its way along the border that delineates the garden from the field opposite, running off the hill behind, an asparagus fern scrambling up and over its banks. Lower down we find branches that have been cut back and died; we have the idea to use both the fresh living stems as well as the dried ones.

Using a large kenzan in the base of the bowl, I fix the pomegranate branches to this first. They are layered with glossy bronze-green leaves and scarlet flowers, some developing into the red-brown spherical fruits. I position them in an asymmetric 'L' shape, with the flowers towards the centre. Next the asparagus fern – the dark green makes the fresh stems appear slightly heavier so we place these at the bottom, with the sunbleached ones reaching upwards and outwards. Lastly the papery globes of *Scabiosa* seedpods, and a few of the fresh flowers, scattered in an arc away from the centre.

In Greece, it is tradition for a houseguest to bring a pomegranate as a gift when visiting the new home of a friend for the first time. The word 'pomegranate' derives from 'seeded apple' in medieval Latin. Native to Afghanistan and Iran, it is an important cultural and religious motif around the world, symbolizing prosperity, fertility and abundance.

Field Poppies and Bindweed

Arabian pea (*Bituminaria bituminosa*)
Bladder campion (*Silene vulgaris*)
Cocksfoot (*Dactylis glomerata*)
Drumstick allium (*Allium sphaerocephalon*)
Field poppy (*Papaver rhoeas*)
Field scabious (*Knautia arvensis*)
Jerusalem sage (*Phlomis fruticosa*)
Ribwort plantain (*Plantago lanceolata*)
Rock-rose (*Helianthemum nummularium*)
Sharp rush (*Juncus acutus*)
Spiny starwort (*Pallenis spinosa*)
Wall rocket (*Diplotaxis tenuifolia*)
Woolly bindweed (*Convolvulus languginosus*)

Terracotta vase by Poterie Ravel
Chicken wire

One evening, in that soft, hazy light so particular to the end of the day in Southern France, I gather an armful of all the things I think are evocative of Les Terres de Pierre and the landscape that surrounds it. The small terracotta urn was handmade at Poterie Ravel in Aubagne, one of the oldest family-run ceramics factories in France. Its dusky ochre colour and softly textural handle make terracotta (the direct translation from the Italian is 'baked earth') especially fitting for outdoor arrangements and rustic alfresco dining.

Cool water to the brim and a fist-sized scrunch of chickenwire slotted inside to support the stems. Some light greenery for the base – woody verbena from the garden and the fronds of fennel leaves, which I peel from the stalks and use as a feathery filler, nestled low into the vase. The stone passage fills with the intoxicating aromatics of lemon and aniseed. I layer in a mixed assemblage of foraged flowers and grasses by variety but in no particular order. The colours are desaturated by the lowering sun and appear almost dusty. In goes the forked stems of Arabian pea at varying heights, then drumstick allium, bladder campion, spires of Jerusalem sage and wall rocket, with the field scabious dotted throughout. Next the shorter stems of starwort, rock-rose, pale pink bindweed and a trio of translucent field poppies, dipped in just-boiled water for a few seconds before they are gently lowered into the vase (to help keep them perky). To finish, a few wild grasses including the common weed ribwort plantain. The oval inflorescences contain hundreds of seeds encircled by a halo of tiny tan flowers.

OPPOSITE
Early evening in Provence calls for a glass of rosé and the slow, mindful arrangement of wildflowers.

AN IRREVERENT IDYLL
Great Dixter, East Sussex, England
July

We used to visit Dixter long before we knew anything at all about gardening or growing flowers. Now several times a year, these trips have a certain pilgrimage-like feel to them. We don't travel by foot or on horseback, but there is a devotional aspect to the journey itself. Each time we expect to come away enriched, and we always do. My favourite time to visit is the autumn when it is hard to imagine a place more atmospheric. The gardens are wreathed in mist in the morning and at the end of the day the scent of a bonfire drifts between the topiary.

Dixter was the home of the idiosyncratic gardener and writer Christopher Lloyd (1921-2006). Christo, as he was known to his friends, grew up here and after boarding school, Modern Languages at Cambridge, short spells in India and East Africa during World War II and a degree in horticulture at Wye, he returned home and spent the rest of his life devoted to the garden. He wrote twenty-five books and was a contributor to many publications including a popular weekly column in *Country Life* magazine for over forty years.

Christo came to the garden as a young man when the skeleton was fully formed and the structure well established. He spent the next fifty years putting 'flesh on the bones'. His father's mania for

PREVIOUS
Jess (left) and Ally (right) contemplating the mouthwateringly vibrant Long Border at Great Dixter in high summer.

OPPOSITE
Making a start. Refining a recipe of ingredients from any summer garden (let alone Dixter!) can be a daunting task. If in doubt, take a walk.

topiary resulted in dense geometric hedging, box and yew, as well as meticulously pruned fighting cocks, blackbirds, pheasants and coffee pots (all since morphing into peacocks). A myriad of garden rooms, individually defined by the lusciously thick green walls, open out one after the other, encircling the house and spiralling outwards to meet the surrounding countryside.

Ideas are what make Dixter such an addictive and infectious place to be. The garden is world famous but it is as much about the energy and enthusiasm of the people as it is the plants. The design has continually evolved under the stewardship of Fergus Garrett who was mentored by Christo – they worked together collaboratively from 1992 until his death. As his successor, Fergus has continued to hone, elaborate and experiment; Dixter is a magnet for people greedy for knowledge and has bred a culture of community, from the team of enthusiastic gardeners, scholars, students and volunteers to its adoring public.

It's a worthy pursuit to celebrate the places we love, taking inspiration and then enfolding this into whatever artistic medium it is that we practice ourselves. There are many overlapping threads in garden and floral design and over the past ten years Great Dixter has been, for us, a conduit to exploring and deepening our understanding

of what these are. It is responsible for many growing and arranging experiments with material combinations, colour and texture (some more successful than others) and the adoption of innumerable plants that we encountered there for the first time, now happily rooted in the soil of our Hampshire cutting garden – angel's fishing rod (*Dierama pulcherrimum*), Korean burnet (*Sanguisorba hakusanensis* 'Lilac Squirrel'), fire lily (*Crocosmia* 'Hellfire'), yellow meadow rue (*Thalictrum flavum* subsp. *glaucum*).

Today is the first of July and I unpack my kit in the Hovel, an old cowshed between the topiary lawn and The Old Rose Garden. It's a blustery summer morning, with a heavy, overcast sky of low cloud that is making Jess a little cross. Clipping the worn leather holster to my belt and making sure I'm armed with snips, I'm suddenly overwhelmed by the prospect of where to begin. This is a new sensation for me – as an event florist I am used to turning up in unfamiliar places and having to think on my feet. To spend twelve hours picking and arranging at Great Dixter is surely on the bucket list of any flower lover. But now, standing in the shadow of the barn I'm momentarily at a loss. To try to 'capture' the spirit of this garden in a flower arrangement suddenly seems a ludicrous proposition. I should have prepared; I should have refined what I'm doing, or know where to start at least. But I know this

OPPOSITE LEFT
On the threshold of one of the world's greatest gardens.

OPPOSITE RIGHT
A bizarre mix, but it works. Field poppies, bright pink snapdragons and honesty seedpods.

ABOVE LEFT
A view of the house from the High Garden.

ABOVE RIGHT
A stately stem of meadow rue (*Thalictrum flavum* subsp. *Glaucum*) towers above architectural leaves and dainty daisy-faces.

is irrational. The whole idea of being here is to arrange flowers in an entirely spontaneous way – to discover new varieties, to experiment, to be in that place, in the moment, without any prior planning. Fixating on the creation of a preconceived 'design' is not the point.

I have to battle this out in my own mind as Jess has disappeared into the undergrowth grumbling about light levels. Just then a gardening intern walks over to introduce himself – Naciim Benkreira, Ruth Borun Scholar, from Washington DC. I tell him of my dilemma. 'What on earth am I going to do?' I say. It's a rhetorical question but one that Naciim seems prepared to answer. 'Dixter is all about the little moments', he says. 'If in doubt, take a walk.' So that is what I do.

RIGHT
A living, ever-changing tapestry of plants at Great Dixter.

OPPOSITE
A selection of choice, freshly cut stems awaiting arrangement in the Hovel.

FINDING FLOWERS
Rules Were Made to be Broken

When you arrive at Great Dixter you step through the front gate onto a stone path flanked by wildflower meadows. Straight ahead is the medieval porch at the base of which a potted display evolves season by season. This is what you hurry towards, to see what is new, because there is always something unexpected and interesting in the way it has been put together that usually incites strong opinions – the first talking point. But before you get there, you spy The Sunk Garden, down some steps under a dense yew archway, crammed with exuberant planting. It beckons, then tugs you over. You veer to the right, tunnel in and are swallowed whole.

It is a week past midsummer and the garden is a boiling, churning ocean of plants in every shape, size and shade imaginable. Following the narrow flagstone paths, brushing our hands along the texture of the evergreen walls it's a journey of constant stop-starts – the scribbling of notes, taking of photographs, phones out to identify new varieties. Giant leaves abut miniature pines. Bright poppies vibrate against one another, competing for vibrancy. We pause to covet a particularly delicious *Mathiasella bupleuroides* 'Green Dream' beneath ghostly spires of bear's breeches (*Acanthus mollis*) (✱), twiggy spurge (*Euphorbia* × *pseudovirgata*) (✻), to admire an arching silver stem of angel's fishing rod (*Dierama pulcherimum*) (✾) and the slender spires of rampion bellflower (*Campanula rapunculus*) (✱). Clashing colours abound – red ladybird poppies (*Papaver* 'Ladybird') among fluffy pink cornflowers (*Centaurea cyanus* 'Pink Ball') (✻). Tastefully subtle colours – the crinkled petals of stormy field poppies (*Papaver rhoeas* 'Amazing Grey') (✾) – keep company with gaudier neighbours such as the recurring large-flowered evening primrose (*Oenothera glazioviana*) (✽).

The plants spill and spar, collide and creep. Stems embrace, petals dip and dance, seed heads jitter. In every square metre there is an almost unbelievable quantity of botanical treasure – intruiging pairings, startling colours, surprising behaviour. It's beautiful, so beautiful. But it isn't easy, and it isn't polite either. In some places the planting is overwhelming. There are unusual bedfellows and the occasional affront. Christo referred to good taste in an interview as a 'swear word'. No – this is a garden that coaxes and cajoles (and sometimes arm-twists). It challenges us to inspect, to question, to want to learn more. It seems to dare us to open our eyes and our minds to new ideas. Dixter is a sort of living essay of plants and human endeavour. It's a plantsman's paradise, a garden of trial and analysis, conceptual debate and experimentation. It's charming and cheeky, weird and wonderful – and if you love plants you are quickly drunk and delirious.

Lilac Squirrel and Daylily

Angel's fishing rod (*Dierama pulcherrimum* 'Blackbird' and 'Pink Rocket')
Cornflower (*Centaurea cyanus* 'Red Ball')
Cranesbill (*Geranium* 'Dragon Heart')
Daylily (*Hemerocallis* 'Corky')
Evening primrose (*Oenothera biennis*)
Hairy chervil (*Chaerophyllum hirsutum* 'Roseum')
Korean burnet (*Sanguisorba hakusanensis* 'Lilac Squirrel')
Lemonbalm (*Melissa officinalis*)
Meadowsweet (*Filipendula ulmaria*)
Meadow rue (*Thalictrum flavum*)
Perfoliate alexanders (*Smyrnium perfoliatum*)
Sweet William catchfly (*Silene armeria*)
Tobacco flower (*Nicotiana* 'Whisper')
Tree mallow (*Malva* × *clementii* 'Rosea')
Umbrella milkwort (*Tolpis barbata*)
Wood fern (*Dryopteris* - variety unknown)

Vintage ceramic vase with handles
Chicken wire

PREVIOUS LEFT
Arranging an assemblage of flowers from Dixter's richly complex and biodiverse meadows, paying particular attention to rhythm, repetition, and movement.

PREVIOUS RIGHT
The strange alchemy of meadow grasslands, abundant with wildflowers that are crucial to healthy, functioning ecosystems.

OPPOSITE
A composition of warm and cool pinks and yellows, a colour combination loved by the garden's creator.

Yellow and pink is a colour combination that is synonymous with Great Dixter. Christo enjoyed being adventurous with colour and was a vocal advocate of knowing how to break the rules. This arrangement was a challenge, and to make it I had to force myself out of my comfort zone. I wouldn't naturally be tempted to pair cold pink with sulphur and chartreuse, but the addition of the rusty brown alexanders helped me to bridge the two and subdue the overall effect. The experiment taught me a lot about using different values of a colour. It might be my favourite arrangement of the year.

I choose an Arts and Crafts ceramics vase for the timber framed porch - tall, with scrolled double handles on either side. Two chicken wire cushions are stacked inside. First the ferns go in as a collar, angled in varying directions so as not to appear too uniform. Then a layer of the perfoliate alexanders and the lemonbalm. I now have a bronze and lime foliage base and the surface of the vase is filled. For the shape - tree mallow and meadow rue for height and the Korean burnet 'Lilac Squirrel' for width. I use the cool custard-yellow daylily as a focal point, which links to the earthy tones of the ferns with its bronze reverse petals. The meadowsweet adds creamy clouds of fluffy texture and the remaining flowers are peppered throughout at varying heights. I save the best till last - a few prized stems of angel's fishing rod. Glinting in the dim light of the porch they are like adding jewelry, the final touch.

Daisy and Dropwort En Plein Air

Bamboo (*Bambusa vulgaris*)
Buttercup (*Ranunculus repens*)
Knapweed (*Centaurea nigra*)
Ox-eye daisy (*Leucanthemum vulgare*)
Water dropwort (*Oenanthe pimpinelloides*)
Yellow rattle (*Rhinanthus minor*)

Ceramic footed dish by Noe Kuremoto
Kenzan

Wandering the garden, I'm inspired to make a sliver of the meadow in this white ceramic bowl. The vessel is well suited to a minimal arrangement and, because of the width of the dish, can take some height. The wooden bench under the mulberry tree afforded a workbench and a view over the Upper Moat and Topiary Lawn from where I selectively chose a handful of stems to make this site-specific design. There are over a dozen individual meadow habitats at Dixter, providing a high degree of biodiversity. The meadows blur the boundaries of the garden, smudging them into the wider landscape, and they are as quintessentially 'Dixter' as the famed Long Border.

I fix a triangular kenzan into the dish so that I can add the ingredients to appear as if they are growing up from one small cutaway, leaving the rest of the surface of the bowl, and the water within it, still visible. I start with the tallest stems and work my way down to the bowl creating an outline pyramid form. The concentration this takes, to securely place each stem, means it is a methodical, slow and meditative process, especially with the strip of meadow undulating behind. A windfall mulberry falls from the overhanging tree and lands beside me – a gift of the passing breeze. It tastes of summer.

OPPOSITE
An asymmetric, pyramid-shaped arrangement inspired by the Orchard meadow at Dixter, which spills into the surrounding landscape.

Yellow rattle is a semi-parasitic plant; by leeching nutrients from the root systems of the surrounding grasses, it allows less robust wildflowers an opportunity to thrive.

Angel's Fishing Rod, Sorrel, Milky Bellflower

Angel's fishing rod (*Dierama pulcherrimum* 'Blackbird')

Burnet (*Sanguisorba tenuifolia* var. *Alba*)

Crocosmia 'Lucifer'

Farewell to spring (*Clarkia amoena*, 'Memoria')

Hedge bedstraw (*Gallium mollugo*)

Hydrangea macrophylla 'Nikko Blue'

Hydrangea serrata 'Bluebird'

Meadow rue (*Thalictrum delavayi*)

Milky bellflower (*Campanula lactiflora* 'Prichard's Variety')

Parsley (*Petroselinum crispum*)

Perfoliate alexanders (*Smyrnium perfoliatum*)

Plantain lily (*Hosta* 'Blue Cadet')

Poppy (*Papaver rhoeas* 'Amazing Grey')

Queen Anne's lace (*Ammi majus*)

Red sorrel (*Rumex acetosella*)

Snapdragon (*Antirrhinum majus* 'Potomac Lavender')

Wand loosetrife (*Lythrum virgatum* 'Dropmore Purple')

Antique footed bowl in terracotta

Kenzan

Chicken wire

The Hovel seems sunken into the Topiary Lawn on one side, with the Exotic Garden and Orchard on the other. Gloriously shadowy with a low-slung slit of sidelight, it is a rustic setting for an earthy vessel – a footed terracotta bowl with an aged, mottled patina. There is a perceptible greed for plants at Great Dixter that we identify with and I think – or hope – that our arrangements display a similar lustfulness when it comes to ingredients. There is a place for restraint and there is a place for indulgence and to create a garden-inspired arrangement at Great Dixter is to yield to voracity.

In my bucket is a piggish quantity of ingredients in a predominantly cool palette of mauve, lilac and denim blues. I use a kenzan with a chicken wire buffer and create a fan shape, using the larger and darker flower heads lowest, interspersed with the bronze alexanders and touches of meadow rue; the tiny lilac balls have a peppery, lightening effect. Dixter taught us to add a dash of red to enliven a composition that feels a little too safe, and introduced us to growing *Crocosmia*. Among the misty interfusion of cool tones I add a splash of 'Lucifer'.

OPPOSITE
Cool pinks and blues offset by strands of warm, earthy brown and a dash of spicy tabasco red.

STILL LIFE
Charleston Farmhouse, East Sussex, England
July

Charleston Farmhouse is nestled comfortably in the lee of the Sussex South Downs. A handsome Georgian house, it was originally built in the 17th century and in 1916 became the country home to the painters Vanessa Bell and Duncan Grant on a long lease. They remained here for the rest of their lives, in that time producing an astonishing body of work as well as decorating every inch of the farmhouse.

Over the years Charleston was increasingly frequented by a bunch of radical artists, writers and intellectuals who became known collectively as the Bloomsbury Group. The friends were synonymous with a certain blue-stocking bohemianism and a free-spirited way of living and working that cast off the conventional norms of the period. Vanessa was married to art critic Clive Bell but at the time of her move to Sussex they had amicably separated and Vanessa had fallen in love with Duncan. Since Duncan was a conscientious objector they relocated from London to Sussex with Vanessa's two young sons, Julian and Quentin and Duncan's lover, David ('Bunny') Garnett - so that the two could work as farm labourers. In 1918 Duncan and Vanessa had a child, Angelica. She was raised as Clive Bell's daughter and only discovered her true parentage aged eighteen. In 1942, aged twenty-four, she married David Garnett. Vanessa Bell's sister Virginia Woolf and her husband Leonard lived nearby and regular visitors to Charleston included Roger Fry, Maynard Keynes, and Lytton Strachey. Vanessa and Clive Bell never divorced and remained friends until her death at Charleston in 1961.

PREVIOUS
Charleston Farmhouse, flanked by hollyhocks and urns designed by Quentin Bell, planted with red geranium.

OPPOSITE
In a letter to her son Julian in the summer of 1936 Vanessa Bell wrote: 'I must say it has been rather amazing here this week. The house seems full of young people in very high spirits, laughing a great deal at their own jokes...lying about in the garden which is simply a dithering blaze of flowers and butterflies and apples.'

Vanessa and Duncan began decorating the interiors of the house almost immediately after they arrived and they never really stopped. Painting was compulsive and nothing was off limits, from canvases they moved seamlessly on to the walls, the furniture and just about any object with a surface available to decorate – waste-paper baskets, mantels, jugs, screens, beds, lampshades, door frames, even the bath and gramophone. They also designed textiles and many of the curtains, cushions and carpets were their own creations. The original Bloomsbury Group are now long gone and the house itself a reverently preserved piece of history. The chalky murals around the house have a charming spontaneity to them, many as though they were undertaken on the spur of the moment, without much planning or preparation. Through the brushstrokes you can feel the humanity of the home it once was, full of people and laughter, boredom and turbulence, argument and productivity, music and reading, grief and companionship.

The garden was reworked by Roger Fry from a sparse kitchen garden containing a few apple trees, and continues to evolve today under the head gardener Harry Hoblyn. Heavily influenced by Gertrude Jekyll, Fry designed a walled garden with a formal rectangular structure and narrow gravel paths between the flower beds. The planting was informal, a delirious haze of mixed colours and shapes – a typically English cottage garden – and in summer a melee of roses, lilies, stocks, tobacco flower, apples, plums, hollyhocks, dahlias and heritage pinks. During both wars, the growing of food took priority and the garden produced vegetables and fruit to feed the household.

The Charleston garden is one that I associate with a blissful, carefree sense of repose, with idle hours and tipsiness, amateur dramatics and swirling creative inspiration. This it has certainly been. But there is another side to this garden. In addition to providing pleasure and frivolity, this place cradled a family and group of friends through two world wars and incomprehensible sorrow.

In 1937, Vanessa's adored son Julian was killed driving an ambulance in the Spanish Civil War. He was only twenty-nine. Four years later her sister Virginia Woolf drowned herself in the river Ouse. I wonder whether Vanessa took solace from her garden during these years, whether she knelt in the earth and thought of them while pruning or weeding, whether she walked the paths at night unable to sleep, breathing in the scent of the roses and pinks.

OPPOSITE
Harry Hoblyn, Charleston's head gardener, helps to identify cuttings.

ABOVE
The kitchen garden at Charleston Farmhouse.

FINDING FLOWERS
A Painterly Palette

Both Vanessa and Duncan would pick bunches of flowers from which to paint still lifes. Little is known of Vanessa's precise feelings for flower arranging but I think it's safe to assume she wouldn't have fiddled with her arrangements for long. Her numerous floral paintings show casual groupings, usually of multiple varieties. The flowers are displayed in domestic settings - a balcony, a kitchen table, a console or plinth. Often there is a piece of fruit or two nearby, an open book, a printed textile curtain or tablecloth. My favourites include *Flowers in a Glass Vase* (1930), which depicts a single pink hollyhock with drooping fuschia, sea holly, poppies and dusty miller and *Asters and Hydrangeas* (c.1930s–1940s), featuring a central cardoon head within the arrangement and a glowing quince on the table beside the stoneware jar. This is how I like to arrange flowers at home - off-the-cuff, mixed bunches of whatever is to hand. It is a simple but deeply pleasurable ritual - bringing seasonal tokens indoors to study and enjoy, and it feels fitting here to do just that.

We are given use of the farmhouse kitchen for the day and a stockpile of Quentin Bell vases. The garden is in a state of sweet summer disorder; a rich embroidery of colours are woven through the borders like planted brushstrokes between sculptures and casts. Candy pink rosemallow (*Lavatera trimestris* 'Loveliness') (✽), clouds of red, blue and raspberry, fuschia hollyhock spires (*Alcea rosea*) (✽), dashes of cool yellow and white royal lily (*Lilium regale*) (✽). The zest of marigolds and red-hot pokers fizzle against masses of cornflowers, borage, spires of foxgloves, roses and watery geranium interrupted by cooling pools of silvery cotton thistles, globe artichokes, lavender and clary sage. Vanessa and Duncan loved greygreens and they appear often among the planting scheme in the garden as well as in their paintings.

Sweet Pea, Nasturtium, Poppy Leaf

Cornflower (*Centaurea cyanus* 'Mauve Boy')
Honeysuckle (*Lonicera periclymenum*)
Nasturtium (*Tropaeolum* 'Gleam')
Nasturtium (*Tropaeolum* 'Jewel of Africa')
Opium poppy (*Papaver somniferum*)
Sweet pea (*Lathyrus* 'Albutt Blue')
Sweet pea (*Lathyrus* 'Charlie's Angel')

Vase by Quentin Bell

The vase was designed by Quentin Bell for Fulham Pottery, probably mid-1980s. You can imagine the scent of the honeysuckle and peppery nasturtium picked up on a summer's evening, mingling with cigarette smoke as people wandered out through the French doors into the garden. In the early days, this was a storage room used by Bunny Garnett as a place to store his beekeeping gear, but it later evolved to be used as a drawing room where Duncan and Vanessa would nap in the afternoons and where the assembled company would adjourn after dinner for brandy, huddling around the fireplace in winter. The wallpaper was a paisley pattern by Vanessa Bell that she and Duncan stencilled onto the walls in the 1940s – the white flowers were added individually, by hand.

A garden-gathered posy beside a shabby rose-pink sofa. The simple, narrow-necked vase negates the need for any fuss with mechanics. The sweet peas are placed first in a criss-cross formation to create a grid for the other stems to lean against. I start with the smoky blue peas, which pick up the lavender-grey of the wallpaper, then add poppy leaf, honeysuckle, a sprinkling of the fluffy purple cornflowers and, lastly, a few twirling stems of nasturtium in peach and fiery orange to break up the traditional complementary pairing of purple and yellow.

PREVIOUS LEFT
The fireplace in Duncan Grant's studio at Charleston Farmhouse.

PREVIOUS RIGHT
Jess photographing the painters' garden surrounded by hollyhocks (*Alcea rosea*) and mauve cornflowers (*Centaurea cyanus* 'Mauve Boy').

OPPOSITE
A strong diagonal line is created by the high honeysuckle on the left and low nasturtium on the right in similar colours. The cornflowers are grouped in a congregation towards the centre.

Martagon Lily, Maltese Cross

Curry plant (*Helichrysum italicum*)
Field scabious (*Knautia arvensis*)
Foxglove (*Digitalis* 'Glory of Roundway')
Maltese cross (*Lychnis chalcedonica*)
Martagon lily (*Lilium martagon* 'Claude Shride')
Nasturtium (*Tropaeolum* 'Gleam')
Prairie mallow (*Sidalcea candida* 'Little Princess')
Snapdragon (*Antirrhinum majus* 'Monarch')
Snapdragon (*Antirrhinum majus* 'Potomac Dark Orange')
Sweet pea (*Lathyrus* 'Almost Black')
Sweet pea (*Lathyrus* 'Cupani')
Sweet pea (*Lathyrus* 'Prince of Orange')

Vase by Quentin Bell

Against the muted paint colours behind, a sheaf of red catches a slant of afternoon sun. The distempered green walls of Clive Bell's study are lent a leafy filter, the light dappled through the leaves of a giant magnolia that climbs the front facade of the farmhouse. The arrangement seems to bring a piquant pop to the details of soft, dusky reds around the room, from the faded floor rug to the books and small accents on the fireplace to the art books lining the shelves. The coffee table was custom-made by J.J. Kallenborn, a cabinet maker employed by the Omega workshops, with tiles decorated by Duncan Grant in the 1920s or '30s. This window embrasure was the first surface of Charleston to be painted by Vanessa in 1916–17.

The Charleston garden in a Charleston vase, quickly layered, with little thought to the exact placement of each flower, and no mechanics. It's less than perfect; the lily and snapdragons are visually heavy, the pops of yellow curry plant and almost-black sweet peas a little 'off'. But, like many of Vanessa Bell's floral paintings, there's a certain cottage-garden charm in that and I wonder whether spontaneously made arrangements evoke a sense of vitality and immediacy that sometimes more laboured compositions seem to lack.

OPPOSITE
This arrangement was inspired by some of the spontaneous compositions that appear in Vanessa Bell's floral paintings, where the ingredients were clearly arranged impulsively without an overall design or outline shape in mind – *Flowers* (1930), *Vase of Flowers, Dieppe* (1946) and *Flowers in a Blue Vase* (1951).

Yarrow and Rosemallow in Duncan Grant's Studio

Corncockle (*Agrostemma githago* 'Light Rose')
Curry plant (*Helichrysum italicum*)
Field scabious (*Knautia arvensis*)
Nasturtium (*Tropaeolum* 'Empress of India')
Rosemallow (*Lavatera trimestris* 'Loveliness')
Shirley poppy (*Papaver rhoeas*)
Sweet pea (*Lathyrus odoratus* 'Charlie's Angel')
Sweet pea (*Lathyrus odoratus* 'Maloy')
Sweet pea (*Lathyrus odoratus* 'Monaco')
Trumpet lily (*Lilium regale* 'Album')
Yarrow (*Achillea filipendulina* 'Cloth of Gold')
Yarrow (*Achillea millefolium* 'Lachsschönheit')

Vase by Quentin Bell

OPPOSITE
It's interesting to observe how the colours and shapes of flowers interact with their background setting – here, the pinks, tomato red and lemon enliven the dusky earthiness of the walls and correspondingly affect the energy in the room.

What is interesting about arranging flowers at Charleston is how saturated the colours look against the softly textured painted backdrops. The colours of the garden, brought indoors, seem like a revelation, instantly more exuberant on the interior. Roger Fry designed the studio in place of an old chicken run and it was painted in dark, muddy colours in order to enhance the vibrancy of Duncan and Vanessa's paintings. They worked here together for many years, side by side. You can feel the creative atmosphere in the air – industrious, bickering, conversational or companionably silent but every day, day after day after day; they loved to work. Imagine the scent of linseed oil and turps that would have pervaded this room when they were working and in the winter when it was the warmest room in the house and so became a sociable sitting room. In 1939 this drove Vanessa, who craved light and quiet in which to paint, to move to her own studio at the top of the house.

Opposite, an arrangement inspired by *Mixed Flowers, Charleston* by Vanessa Bell, painted in 1932: a terracotta jar with what looks like a haphazard collection of chrysanthemum, dahlias and gladioli from the garden, placed in front of the gilt studio mirror. I begin with a base of sweet peas and build in clusters of yarrow as a filler. The mallow and poppies are interspersed with smaller details – corncockle, scabious and nasturtium. Two stems of *Achillea* 'Cloth of Gold' are allowed to swoop off to one side and the lustrous white lily to centrally dominate. The accumulation of paraphernalia around the room – tubes of paint, ashtrays and bottles of alcohol, jars and pots, invitations, photographs, newspaper clippings and holiday souvenirs – means there are no available surfaces to place the arrangement on. We set it on a wooden plinth in front of the soil-brown wall, in order to enjoy the reflection in the oval mirror.

HINTERLAND
North Norfolk Coast, England
July

I still remember the impression Norfolk had on me the first time I visited. A friend told me about the owls hooting in the pine forest along Holkham Beach at dusk and I drove north on that recommendation alone. The next year I sent Jess with a long list of precise instructions – where to walk, where to get coffee and ice cream, where to have a pint with a good view of the sunset. Since then we have both become mothers and have been holidaying here together with the kids for several years.

There are times of life when you crave newness and others when the familiar is comforting and more appealing than adventure. Having young children, you want to know in advance how long it takes to get from here to there and there to here. You want to be outside as much as possible. North Norfolk is chartered territory: we habitually revisit the fish smokery, the little pottery place, the pub where you can watch your supper being cooked over a roaring applewood fire, the pick-your-own raspberry field, the quiet beach spots, the farm shop. We know that in July the sun rises at 4am and it isn't dark until gone 9.30pm. We have our favourite walks; we collect shells and pine cones. It feels like a home away from home.

This stretch of the Norfolk coast has a particular character that is all its own. A flat landscape, the skies are wide and the buildings red brick and flint. Many sport the distinctive Dutch gable-ends that migrated across the North Sea with settlers from the Netherlands and Low Countries in the 16th century. The beaches are wild and vast, the dunes spiky with marram grass. At Holkham when the tide is out the sea is only just visible on the horizon. There are aromatic pine woods, tidal saltmarsh, rolling dunes, richly diverse plants and wildlife.

PREVIOUS
The Shell Museum, Glandford.

OPPOSITE
Mission accomplished! Foraging along the coastal path between Moreston and Blakeney.

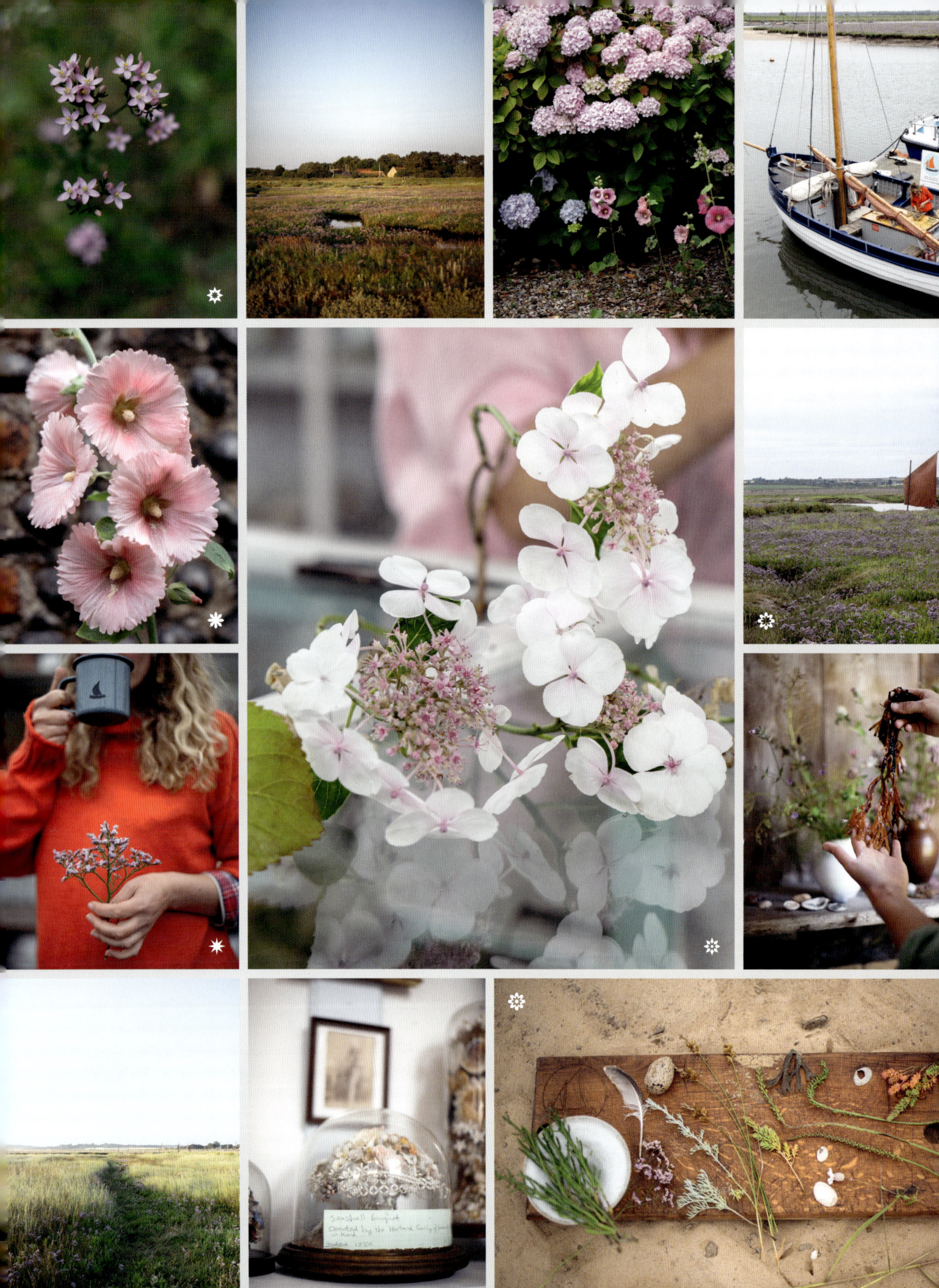

FINDING FLOWERS
Under Sail

In summer the colours are exquisite. Walking from Morston to Blakeney there is a stretching expanse of sea lavender, like a low mist in the space between land and water. This is the first walk we take when we arrive, gazing out over smoky mauve flowers as far as the eye can see. We catalogue the plants along the ridgeway, calling out those we recognize, guessing at those we don't: wild carrot, sea beet, clover, fennel, campion, orache, sea beet, alexanders, lady's bedstraw. Hollyhocks (*Alcea rosea*) run riot through Blakeney (✹) and many of the coastal villages, self-seeding freely and at home in the sandy soil, similarly sugary *Hydrangea* are a common sight in local gardens (✸).

A welcome sight on the watery horizon or in the harbour is the dusky terracotta sail of the Coastal Exploration Company (✸). A small Swallows-and-Amazons fleet of traditional wooden boats including a mussel flat, crab boat and whelk boat patrol this stretch of coastline, taking visitors out under sail to explore the more remote beaches, marshes, islands and creeks. One of the side-effects of our work is that we are never not in the mindset of looking and learning – wherever there are plants there is the chance to explore, to find inspiration, to come across new varieties and witness how they behave, whether in wild places or cultivated. This is one of the wildest places left in the UK and it seemed an opportunity not to miss to experience maritime plants in their native environment.

We set out one morning during a neap tide in a 1965 Brancaster mussel flat, an ex-working boat from Burnham Staithe. Drifting out of Wells harbour into the East Fleet river estuary, a milk-white moon jellyfish undulates past in the water. Swallows swoop overhead and a cold breeze greets us off the sea. The mud flats are clay soil, riddled with creeks and pitted with gilly crab holes. On top it is thickly carpeted with sea lavender (*Limonium vulgare*) (✹) with papery lavender flowers on short branching stems and low growing sea purslane (*Sesuvium portulacastrum*), the crunchy leaves of which can be eaten raw or made into a tangy, salty pesto. As the boat meanders further into the salt marsh towards East Hills the creeks wriggle through the mud, narrowing and widening again, twisting and turning. Our guide, Nick, names the birds we don't recognize – red shank, curlew, common and sandwich terns. We stop on a slim spit of beach for a picnic and sail back past skeletal shapes of disused jetties and a small bridge looming out of the water, remnants of history preserved by the salt. Over a hundred years ago sheep were grazed here. There are spits of oyster beds, miniature forests of samphire (*Crithmum maritimum*) thriving in the salty gloop, sea blite (*Suaeda maritima*), which has branches of glaucous leaves emerging from a submerged rootstock, frosted orache (*Atriplex littoralis*), sea thrift (*Armeria maritima*) (✸), and seaside centaury (*Centaurium littorale*) (✸). We recognize some – sea aster (*Tripolium pannonicum*), sea wormwood (*Artemisia maritima*) and sea campion (*Silene uniflora*) – the salty relatives of those in our own garden.

Sea Lavender, Sea Rush, Sea Blite

Marsh pennywort (*Hydrocotyle vulgaris*)

Sea lavender (*Limonium vulgare*)

Sea rush (*Juncus maritimus*)

Shrubby sea blite (*Suaeda vera*)

Hand thrown ceramic vase from Made in Cley

Made in Cley pottery is one of our favourite local haunts and we were lucky to be allowed to borrow a few pieces during this trip. (Of course, it proved too heart-wrenching to return some and they inevitably made the return journey to the studio in London). For this arrangement from our saltmarsh sail we chose a vase with a creamy glaze flecked with brown speckles. It's an interesting challenge to arrange with unfamiliar materials – particularly when combined with other plants that are natural neighbours in their native environment – and there's a unique excitement in the feeling of handling a new ingredient and seeing how it arranges in a vase.

A small maritime posy: all plants that can tolerate brackish water and sea spray. The shrubby sea blite, otherwise known as sea rosemary, immediately caught our eye; it has a mass of thick woody stems and tiny succulent leaves that have a delicate herby flavour and beautiful variation in the colouring from yellow to blue-green to peachy pink. I include a mix and amongst these dense little branches go a few sprigs of sea lavender. The marsh pennywort naturally trails and so is obliged to cascade in a downwards trajectory. A few thin, graceful stems of sea rush with tufted bronze flowers catch the light.

OPPOSITE
Arranging the unfamiliar – foraged wildflowers and foliage from along the North Norfolk coastline.

Susie's Hydrangea, Bracken and Roses

Bracken (*Pteridium aquilinum*)
Garden roses (varieties unknown)
Honeysuckle (*Lonicera periclymenum*)
Japanese anemone (*Anemone × hybrida* 'Robustissima')
Red valerian (*Centranthus ruber*)
'Susie's hydrangea' (variety unknown)

Bowl from Made in Cley
Kenzan

OPPOSITE
Finding similarities in natural forms at the Shell Museum – flowers, fishbones, feathers, shells and coral.

OVERLEAF
The wild beauty of the saltmarsh. Early morning, North Norfolk.

The Shell Museum in Glandford is a rare curiosity. It was built in 1915 specifically to house an extensive collection of seashells, birds' eggs, fossils and artefacts from the local area amassed over a sixty-year period by Sir Alfred Jodrell, a local philanthropist who also built the neighbouring church. The museum interiors are exquisite, decorated in pale sugared-almond colours – light blue, white and gold – with iridescent shells everywhere you look. There is no overtly floral connection here except that this is a place that has been created solely for the appreciation of natural beauty; in this respect, the displaying of shells is very much like the arrangement of flowers.

I'm taking inspiration from the curving asymmetric ornamentation of the Rococo period, during which the natural motif of a shell was a familiar emblem. I select a fan-shaped ceramic bowl at the pottery in Cley and materials that evoke the natural beauty of objects you might find while beachcombing. Garden roses and hydrangea have a shell-like quality, ferns are reminiscent of fish bones and feathers, honeysuckle and valerian of coral and seaweed. A kind neighbour across the lane from our holiday cottage allows us to pillage a few stems from the abundant lacecap hydrangea outside her cottage and the roses are snipped from the museum garden – in both cases the exact variety name is unknown but it is similar to *Hydrangea macrophylla* 'Veitchii' and 'Teller White'. I use a kenzan in the base of the bowl to enable me to create a strong outline in the shape of a scallop shell, with the flowers fanning outwards from one point. The watery background and rusted metal chest seem to call for a braver splash of colour among the sorbet tones – a fiery orange, deep red and hot pink instantly inject a sense of drama into this tranquil space.

'I have got a new madness, I am running wild after shells ... the beauty of shells is as infinite as flowers.' Mrs Delaney (1700–1788) was a botanical artist and famous shell decorator; floral shellworks were extremely popular in 18th- and 19th-century England.

FINDING FLOWERS
Hortus Conclusus

Wiveton Hall is a Jacobean manor between Blakeney and Cley-next-the-Sea. Built in 1652 it is an enchanting house, with flint walls and Dutch gables, home to the McCarthy family.

We never met Chloe, who was a keen plantswoman and largely responsible for the charm of the garden; she died aged 102, a year before I first visited. On a perfect summer's day we walk around the grounds with her son, Desmond, who has lived here all his life.

We step out of the house into the sunken garden, created in the early 1900s and cross to admire a robust California tree poppy (*Romneya coulteri*) in the far corner, smothered with crinkled white flowers. Desmond points out a yellow jasmine that his mother brought back as a cutting from the palace gardens in Madrid and, later, the *Agapanthus* his father introduced after a trip to South Africa. He is clearly fond of these links to the past – the vestiges of pre-war gardening like the Edwardian box topiary (at that time the gardens here required eight gardeners to care for them) and the way the plants have self-sown since. He gestures a faded tweed sleeve to a few looming spires of evening primrose, *Erigeron* spilling from the cracks between stones, the tapers of foxgloves going to seed and the 'beautiful but dastardly' valerian atop the flint walls. Below the house we push through dense overgrowth beside a pond of black water backed by Japanese knotweed. Walking ahead, Desmond mutters that this always reminds him of a painting by Henri Rousseau (*The Snake Charmer*, 1907) and I can see the association – there is something tropical and dangerous about the atmosphere of this dark corner. But then we come to the kitchen garden (✱), walls lined with espaliered apple, plum and pear. This was Chloe's domain and here she grew flowers, fruits, vegetables and herbs. The gardener, Amanda, remembers Chloe's love of naturalistic planting and how she intentionally left weeds for the sake of biodiversity. 'In many ways, she was ahead of her time', she says. Beyond the walls, flat saltwater marshes stretch a mile to the North Sea. The dark shapes of Monterey pines are silhouetted against a dazzling blue sky.

'I don't know what you'll find', Desmond quips as we ready our kit – the usual jumble of wire, snips, buckets and an odd assortment of vases. I lean over to show him my 'shopping list', scribbled down during the morning. 'Good luck to you' is his reply and he wanders off looking sceptical. It is only afterwards that I realize how unintelligible and deranged my notes may appear: *White strawberry?? Winter savoury! Seaweed (underlined) – weird mix with herbs? Fuschia with variegated peony leaves (PINK). Circaea (sorcery?), poss. with witchy branch...* Ideas come thick and fast when I'm choosing ingredients; the generosity of being given free reign among someone else's plants somehow makes the selection process pleasurable and agonizing in equal measure. You don't want to take too much but there are tempting vistas everywhere – a healthy, established *Fuschia* with branches overarching the lane (✸), swathes of peonies, the flowers a few weeks gone but leaves fading to pink at the edges.

Hollyhock, Spent Sorrel, Sea Kale

Hollyhock (*Alcea rosea* 'Nigra', 'Chater's Double Pink', other varieties unknown)

Sea kale (*Crambe maritima*)

Sorrel (*Rumex acetosa*)

Wild carrot (*Daucus carota*)

Yellow daylily (*Hemerocallis lilioasphodelus*)

Hand-thrown ceramic vase from Made in Cley

You can't come to Norfolk without noticing the triffid-like hollyhocks lining the village streets and gardens – they are utterly redolent of the English seaside in summer. Hollyhocks easily cross-pollinate so the colours can be a surprise from one year to the next. In the hall at Wiveton is a portrait of the daughter of 'pretty, witty Nell' Gwyn, the mistress of King Charles II. She wears an apricot sash, and is flanked by chairs lined in pink satin. The wooden chest below the portrait is vacant and seems a suitably welcoming space for a large bouquet.

All from the walled kitchen garden and the lane leading up to it – a large armful of hollyhocks in vibrant pink, pale yellow and a glossy dark chocolate. From these I strip the rusty leaves and sear them in just-boiled water for a minute, until the stream of bubbles cease. I place them in the narrow-necked vase first to create a large 'V' shape and intersperse with stems of wild carrot and sorrel, which has a delicate pinkish tinge to the seeds, with a cluster of the silvery sea kale at the base. Arranging these leathery leaves always makes me think of the florist Constance Spry, who democratized the use of unusual and undervalued botanical materials. Fond of weeds, hedgerow foraging and pillaging the kitchen garden for the leaves of kale, chard, rhubarb and cabbages, she shunned the primness of traditional floristry and was responsible for the resurgence of a looser aesthetic that put the ingredients in pride of place.

PREVIOUS LEFT
An enticing village alleyway with garden roses, hollyhocks and red valerian.

PREVIOUS RIGHT
Hollyhock (*Alcea rosea* 'Halo Apricot').

OPPOSITE
Hollyhocks are stately and theatrical, ideal for arrangements that are intended to make an impact or for high-ceilinged rooms.

Fox-and-Cubs with Witchy Branches

Cranesbill (*Geranium pratense*)
Fox-and-cubs (*Pilosella aurantiaca*)
Red-flowered bladder senna (*Colutea orientalis*)
Sea buckthorn (*Hippophae rhamnoides*)
Welsh poppy (*Papaver cambricum*)

Hand-thrown ceramic vase from Made in Cley
Chicken wire

We couldn't be more excited to discover this magnificent shrub with the unfortunate name of 'bladder senna' on the lane at Wiveton. A magnificent, cloud-like display of wildly beckoning branches covered in copper-red pea-like flowers. As a gestural branch it ticks every box – long, curving stems, elegantly feathery leaves in an attractive blue-green, intriguing decorative blooms which are followed by papery seedpods in the autumn. Walking along the North Norfolk coast you'll inevitably notice the dense barrier hedges of sea buckthorn with its distinctive silvery-green foliage, smothered in orange berries.

I use the spindly *Colutea* branches first, leaving them tall, and add a couple of stems of the sea buckthorn (thorns removed) lower down. The delicate fox-and-cubs have clusters of rich orange florets above russet buds and a naturally curving shape to the stems, I use these to either side. The scrunched neon tissue of a Welsh poppy and blushing geranium leaves 'on the turn'. Using foliage that is fading or mottled adds a naturalistic look to arrangements and nods to a discernable change in the season; in July we notice the first clues that late summer is wending its inevitable way towards us. This vase is one of my favourites for home – the narrow ceramic cylinder is perfect for hastily layered arrangements of branches or grasses.

OPPOSITE
Even with minimal ingredients it is possible to make an impact, provided they are well chosen. Here, the orange poppy, berries and floral tassels echo the warmth of the gold gilt on the picture frames behind.

White Strawberry, Fuschia and Tree Poppy

African lily (*Agapanthus* - variety unknown)
California tree poppy (*Romneya coulteri*)
Foxglove beardtongue (*Penstemon* 'Apple Blossom')
Fuchsia (variety unknown)
Garden phlox (*Phlox paniculata* 'Pink Eye Flame')
Mexican fleabane (*Erigeron karvinskianus*)
Peony (*Paeonia* - variety unknown)
Rose (*Rosa* - variety unknown)
Sage (*Salvia greggii* 'Royal Bumble')
Welsh poppy (*Papaver cambricum*)
White strawberry (*Fragaria* - variety unknown)

Vase borrowed from Desmond - it belonged to his late mother, Chloe
Chicken wire

'Ah good, you've found the flower room', Desmond calls, catching me out in the process of pilfering the treasure trove of vases. One of the delights of the English country house is that they once had rooms dedicated to the arrangement of flowers, and were stuffed with interesting containers, from ceramics to glassware, pewter gravy jugs, pinholders and occasionally the odd dusty dome of oasis foam. Invariably these are now shared with the booze fridge, dog bed, welly boots and fishing rods, but they are always worth a rummage. The unbridled joy of cutting straight from the garden is sometimes having the freedom to 'pick and mix' from as many plants as possible. Since much of the Wiveton planting was established several decades ago, many of the plant labels have been lost and we are unable to identify the exact varieties.

A borrowed vase for the entrance hall at Wiveton - shadowy and sunken as though it has relaxed into the landscape with a comfortable sigh. I squeeze a little ball of chicken wire in for stem support. The *Fuchsia* acts as a structural branch; I use it to create width and so that the pendulous flowers can dangle in the negative space to either side. This is followed by the tree poppy and then the other flowers. To finish - a few of those turning-pink peony leaves, frail stems of fleabane and a clutch of nodding white strawberries.

OPPOSITE
Pick and mix - a little bit of everything offset by the faintly musical 'earrings' of dangling *Fuschia*.

FOOD & FLOWERS
Edinburgh, Scotland
August

We leave London on a sultry summer's morning, arriving in Edinburgh at lunchtime where it is refreshingly cooler. Our destination is Sciennes Road, between Newington and Marchmont, where there is a glossy green-fronted tenement building – the studio of food stylist, cook and author Jess Elliott Dennison. Jess has written four cookbooks. The latest, *Midweek Recipes*, is self-published and already the most well-thumbed in my kitchen. As a working mother with a toddler, I reach for the quick, deliciously nutritious recipes most evenings. We met on Instagram and got talking – the rest is history.

Jess's studio, Elliott's, has evolved over the years. A few doors up, it was a neighbourhood cafe between 2018 and 2023 with a weekly changing seasonal menu popular for its excellent food and homely feel. The studio – previously a newsagent – came in 2020. Not the best timing to take on a new premises in the middle of a pandemic, but Jess soon turned it into a general store selling everything from flour to olive oil, candles to wine and salt. It is here that she writes and photographs her cookbooks, hosts seasonal supper clubs and teaches cookery demos.

The studio space on Sciennes Road feels like an extension of Jess's home and radiates a cheerful productiveness. Sensitively modernized, it retains its Victorian character – a beautiful wooden floor and period details in the plasterwork, cornicing and elaborate central ceiling rose. The walls are a soft apple green with shaker pegs occasionally displaying a wicker basket or linen towel. Every detail has been carefully curated without feeling over-styled – the brass taps over the carved stone sink in the back, the selection of ceramics and homewares on the shelves – and there are personal touches everywhere, pinned up photos and wonky cafe curtains.

PREVIOUS
À table! The heady marriage of cheese, wine and flowers at Jess Elliott Dennison's studio in Edinburgh.

OPPOSITE
The exquisite mange-tout pea (*Pisum sativum* 'Shiraz') grown by Pyrus Botanicals.

BELOW LEFT
Flowers the colours of honey, peach and caramel.

BELOW RIGHT
A glass of La Vie en Orange by Maison François Ducrot and a coffee floribunda rose (*Rosa* Mokarosa 'Frywitty').

OPPOSITE
Edible detritus: viola, blackcurrant leaf, blackberry and rose petals.

It's early August and we're collaboratively hosting a day of food and flowers at Elliott's. Jess is modest about her flowers but I love her arrangements, always seasonal and often from the garden. Her cooking is similarly unfussy and we share a belief that, with good ingredients, 'technique' is best uncomplicated. We both have very small independent family businesses where everyone pitches in, there is a heavy emphasis on the hand-made and enjoyment of the process is valued over the end result. This day is about celebrating the joy of arranging garden flowers, cooking, eating and convivial conversation. Guests include a dried flowers and coffee shop owner with a love of terrariums, a florist and flower farmer with a walled garden in Perthshire, a mother and daughter who love arranging flowers and are enjoying a day out together, an academic biologist from Glasgow and a Glaswegian accountant who has recently discovered a passion for growing.

For breakfast, sitting around the long communal table, there are madeleines, cherries and treacle fig tea loaf served with salted butter and wafer-thin slivers of Alp Blossom cheese. While I demo an arrangement, Jess gives us tips on her informal but generous hosting style – tearing rather than slicing herbs and ripe fruit, and instead of dicing vegetables, 'drunkenly chopping' them into randomly hewn chunks to show off their shapes and colours. The space smells so good that every dog in the neighbourhood pops their snout round the (always ajar) door to have a good sniff.

The Lunch Menu

'Bloody Mary' salad – tomatoes dressed with
wild garlic, vinegar, kimchi juice and oregano

Baked 'Baron Bigod' – a British artisan cheese,
similar in consistency to brie, with good bread

Olives braised with artichokes,
lemon peel, chilli and fennel

Charred courgettes in lemon and yoghurt

Aioli and mustard-dressed green beans

Doughnut peach and basil salad

Green salad dressed in salsa verde

Blackcurrant fool
(fruit stolen from Jess's husband – sorry Phillip!)

BELOW
Marion Blythe Sandwith of Ochre Botanical Studios with small-flowered foxglove (*Digitalis parviflora* 'Milk Chocolate').

OPPOSITE
A corner of the Elliott's studio, decorated with stoneware vases of viola.

OVERLEAF
Perusing the 'Rosie' tunnel with Fiona Inglis at the Pyrus Botanicals walled garden.

FOOD & FLOWERS

FINDING FLOWERS
A Victorian Walled Garden

We're supplied with flowers for the day by Fiona Inglis of Pyrus Botanicals. I met Fiona in London almost ten years ago. We haven't seen each other since, but Jess and I remain inspired by her dedication to strictly seasonal design and incredibly talented way with colour and texture. We make our way out to East Saltern just outside Pencaitland by taxi, the driver regaling us with stories of his five years as a florist. He most loved doing funerals, he says, and for a late friend, who enjoyed drinking and smoking he created memorial arrangements of bronze and white chrysanthemums carved into the shapes of a pint of Tennent's and a cigarette. With this image hovering in the back of our minds we arrive at the garden of Pyrus, and step into another world.

The walled garden is two and three-quarter acres, enclosed by huge buttresses and red brick walls. Once the kitchen garden to the main house, Saltern Hall, the sheer height and thickness of the walls is indicative of how wealthy the original owner was. The Victorians used the space productively to grow fruit and vegetables, maximizing the space to supply the house with fresh produce. Over the years it has continually evolved, being, at various times, part-orchard, sheep grazing and a Christmas tree plantation. 'You can see that in the earth – the ground within the garden is incredibly diverse', Fiona says. Over coffee and strawberries, she tells us how work started in the garden, taking out some of the trees and levelling off the site to make an experimental and biodynamic market garden. There are still many heritage apple trees, areas given over to wild grass and willowherb, trial beds to see what will grow well – what the stem lengths will be, how the plant will behave in the soil.

Fiona's four polytunnels are named 'Sweaty Betty,' 'Rosie', 'Al' and 'Julio'. In the rose tunnel are the most exquisite velvety blooms in creams, coffee, gold and bronze including 'Vidal Sassoon', 'Julia's Rose' and 'Mokarosa' (✻). Around the perimeter, thick wild borders and native hedging have been left and are teeming with wildlife – feral bees, 'Otis the Stoat' and ducks that return every year to have their babies in safety and seclusion. Before we leave, I can't resist cutting a few stems of raspberry foliage (*Rubus idaeus*) (✣) and creeping thistle (*Cirsium arvense*) (✣). In the afternoon Fiona drives us back into Edinburgh, the back of the van full of flowers. The quality of the materials she grows is exceptional, with interesting varieties and her distinctive eye for blending colour. Among the packed treasures are streaked viola (✻), eye-catching marigolds (*Tagetes*) (✣), tomatoes and peas on the vine and small-flowered foxgloves (*Digitalis parviflora* 'Milk Chocolate') (✣). Every bunch is carefully conditioned and wrapped in brown paper. This is a grower who cherishes every stem.

Aperol Spritz

China aster (*Callistephus chinensis* 'King Size Apricot')

Cornflower (*Centaurea cyanus* 'Classic Fantastic')

Drummond's phlox (*Phlox drummondii* var. *grandiflora* 'Creme Brulee')

French marigold (*Tagetes* 'Burning Embers')

Nasturtium (*Tropaeolum majus* 'Vesuvius' and 'Gleam Salmon')

Mange-tout pea (*Pisum sativum* 'Shiraz')

Pot marigold (*Calendula officinalis* 'Orange Flash')

Rose (*Rosa* 'Honey Dijon')

Snapdragon (*Antirrhinum* 'Appleblossom')

St John's wort (*Hypericum* 'Magical Universe')

Tomato (*Solanum pimpinellifolium* 'Red Currant')

Wild blackberry (*Rubus fruticosus*)

Woolly foxglove (*Digitalis lanata* 'Café Crème')

Tenmoku glaze vase by Cara Guthrie

Chicken wire

PREVIOUS LEFT
The wild border just inside the walled garden is a haven for wildlife.

PREVIOUS RIGHT
Rosa 'Julia's Rose', a delicious coffee-coloured garden rose.

OPPOSITE
Seasonal, organically grown and lovingly crafted by hand – a recipe for success when it comes to food, and flowers.

I love watching cookery demonstrations – in addition to the step-by-step process, you can experience the physicality of gesture and cooking style of the teacher. It is mesmerizing and relaxing to watch the methodical making, and witness their decision-making in real-time. At Elliott's, Jess has a mirror suspended from the ceiling to allow guests to watch her cook during seasonal supper clubs. Before Jess gets started on lunch, I give a practical demonstration of making a flower arrangement for the table.

Table flowers are best kept below the eye-line of diners so as not to interrupt the flow of conversation or break eye-contact across the table. With the exception of a few stems I focus on making a low arrangement sprawling outwards from the 'Honey Dijon' rose. From that warm beige I reel in other ingredients with a yellow-orange undertone. Luminous tomatoes, peach and orange nasturtium veined with red, the apricot-buff of marigold petals, brushed bronze on the reverse. I want to ensure the colour palette doesn't feel too contrived so I add a pop of ice blue and cooler pink – a dash of contrasting temperature helps to liven things up.

Herbalist Nicholas Culpeper called *Calendula* a 'comforter of the heart and spirit'. It was once a popular remedy used in reviving broths and a wreath of marigold flowers hung over the door was believed to protect a home from evil spirits.

Kitchen Garden

Amaranth (*Amaranthus caudatus* 'Coral Fountain')
Apple (*Malus*)
French marigold (*Tagetes patula* 'Burning Embers' and 'Mr Majestic')
Garlic scapes (*Allium sativum*)
Hops (*Humulus lupulus*)
Nasturtium (*Tropaeolum majus* 'Milkmaid')
Mange-tout pea (*Pisum sativum* 'Shiraz')
Pot marigold (*Calendula officinalis* 'Orange Flash')
Raspberry (*Rubus idaeus*)
Tomato (*Solanum pimpinellifolium* 'Red Currant')
Wild blackberry (*Rubus fruticosus*)

Vintage vase borrowed from Jess
Chicken wire

I make a large farm-to-table arrangement for the shop window to welcome guests and show off all the glorious materials we have been supplied with by Pyrus. To celebrate our day of food and flowers, everything in this arrangement is edible. Mid to late summer I incorporate as many fruits and vegetables into designs as possible. They provide a connection between the grower and the table, the food and the flowers. The 'slow food', or 'farm-to-fork' concept is widespread and yet in seasonal restaurants so often the flowers are overlooked – imported and out of context. Today their provenance is afforded prime importance.

I construct the arrangement with a loose outline 'L' shape, using the raspberry, mange-tout and blackberry (with gorgeous gold and khaki berries not yet ripe) as structural branches for height and width. The tallest, straightest ingredient is the allium; this is how they naturally grow and, in a naturalistic arrangement, they look 'right' placed vertically as opposed to very angled or cut short. The flowers are grouped in clusters, growing up through the middle with apples, amaranthus, hops and tomatoes allowed to spill downwards.

OPPOSITE
Good enough to eat – an arrangement of edible materials welcomes guests to a day of food and flowers.

Peaches, Cream and Coffee

Baby's breath (*Gypsophila elegans* 'Covent Garden')
China aster (*Callistephus chinensis* 'King Size Apricot')
Chinese meadow rue (*Thalictrum delavayi*)
Creeping thistle (*Cirsium arvense*)
Largest masterwort (*Astrantia maxima*)
Larkspur (*Delphinium consolida* 'Misty Lavender')
Raspberry (*Rubus idaeus*)
Rosa 'Margaret Merrill'
Rosa 'Mokarosa'
Small-flowered foxglove (*Digitalis parviflora* 'Milk Chocolate')
Smoke bush (*Cotinus coggygria*)
St John's wort (*Hypericum* 'Magical Universe')
Tomato (*Solanum pimpinellifolium* 'Red Currant')
Wild carrot (*Daucus carota* 'Dara')

Tenmoku glaze vase by Cara Guthrie
Chicken wire

The beautiful vases used for the workshop were designed by local ceramicist Cara Guthrie, with a brown-black *tenmoku* glaze. It has the glossy, slightly iridescent surface of black treacle, which amplifies the sense that this concoction of materials is good enough to eat.

When equally enamoured by two colour schemes (provided they work well together and can be blended), I'll often group one on one side and one on the other. I start with the tallest spires to make an asymmetric triangular outline – a dusky mauve larkspur and small foxgloves that are bronze and gold, streaked with fine veins. For foliage I choose the slender, arching stems of raspberry with lime leaves and fruits at varying stages of ripeness and St John's wort with plum leaves and shiny, toffee-coloured flower heads. The coffee-plum fluff of smoke bush and dots of lilac meadow rue are added for textural interest.

OPPOSITE
Blowsy roses and ruffly asters are interspersed with daintier details, tapered spires of foxgloves and larkspur rising above them.

I BLIXEN-STILEN
Rungstedlund, Rungsted, Denmark
August

My fascination with the Danish novelist Karen Blixen began as a teenager. *Out of Africa*, the evocative memoir of her years coffee-farming at the foot of the Ngong Hills (1914–1931) had something of a part to play in leading me to Kenya in the first place, and a formative chapter of my life was focused on returning there – both physically, and, when this was not possible, mentally, through reading, writing and day-dreaming. It felt somehow serendipitous to discover, only a couple of years ago, that Karen Blixen was a prolific flower arranger, and passionate about naturalistic arrangements created from foraged and garden-grown materials. In fact, she is so well-regarded in Denmark that if you walk into a flower shop and ask for a bouquet 'i Blixen-stilen' ('in the Blixen style') they will know exactly what you mean. A collection of essays published in 1992 entitled *Karen Blixen's Flowers: Nature and Art at Rungstedlund* reveals a web of overlapping connections and a philosophy that feels uncannily familiar.

Less than twenty miles north of Copenhagen, Rungstedlund is a low 17th-century inn on the shore of the Danish Oresund coast. Karen Blixen was born in Rungsted and lived here all her life beside the seventeen years she spent in Kenya. In 1931, a few months before she returned to Denmark for good, her former lover Denys Finch-Hatton died when his plane crash-landed at Voi airport. Broken-hearted Karen returned to her birthplace and settled there, spending the next thirty years writing, gardening and arranging flowers. Every evening she would stand on the south-side of the house looking towards Kenya. She once said, 'I have a feeling that wherever I may be in the future, I will be wondering whether there is rain at Ngong'. In the bedroom at Rungstedlund there are two earthenware jugs. Karen brought these

PREVIOUS
The cutting garden and orchard at Rungstedlund, Denmark.

OPPOSITE
An arrangement of pale green hydrangeas and dark red orache by floral decorator Helen Olsen catches the afternoon light against the soft green walls of the study.

back from Africa filled with the red earth of the land she loved, not knowing if she would return (she never did). When she died in 1962 the earth was scattered over her grave. She lies under a huge beech tree close to her faithful German Shepherd, Rommy.

Unusually for a museum, Rungstedlund manages to retain the lived-in and loved atmosphere of a home – there is tinkling jazz, the lighting is dim, the floorboards creak. All the appendages of a historical setting open for public consumption – the souvenir shop and the cafe – are beautifully designed and feel in keeping rather than uncomfortable or exploitative. On each cafe table is a sweet floral gesture in a champagne glass – a few stems of sedum, orache and salvias. In 'Ewald's room' a single red rose is silhouetted against the blue-green walls and the view of the Sound beyond, looking towards Sweden. It is said that the American film director Erling Schroeder, an ardent admirer of Blixen's, sent her a red rose every day during the last year of her life. This ritual is still honoured by the museum today.

RIGHT
A sweet token – one single red rose, hand-picked from the garden in Ewald's room, named after Johannes Ewald, the Danish dramatist, psalm writer and poet, who Karen Blixen liked to imagine stayed and wrote in this room in the 1770s when it was Rungsted Inn.

OPPOSITE
Phlox and snaps – an arrangement 'I Blixen-stilen' above an antique French firescreen. In *Out of Africa* Karen Blixen wrote, 'I had an old wooden screen with painted figures... There in the evenings, when the fire burned clear, the figures would come out, and serve as illustrations to the tales that I told Denys. After I had looked at it for a long time, I folded it up and packed it in a case, wherein the figures might all have a rest for the time being'.

OVERLEAF LEFT
Learning from Helen Olsen, floral decorator at Runstedlund since 1996.

OVERLEAF RIGHT
Snapdragons (*Antirrhinum majus*) galore in the cutting garden – a classic cut flower that blooms all summer, is scented and long-lasting in the vase.

FINDING FLOWERS
Karen's Cutting Garden

We spend the day at Rungstedlund with Helen Olsen, who assumed the position of floral decorator here in 1993 and makes arrangements for the house every Tuesday and Friday. It is a blustery day and between rain showers we follow Helen across the lawn to the west of the house. A white-painted bridge crosses the pond, leading towards an orchard of Victoria plum, cherry, apple and pear trees. The sweet-and-sour late-summer scent of fallen fruit greets us and there is the occasional thunk of windfall in the grass. This garden is tended by volunteers and supplies the house with flowers and foliage throughout the season as it did during Karen's lifetime. Now, in late August, it is abundant with Japanese anemones (*Anemone hupehensis*) (✻), snapdragons, roses and spent hollyhocks, the first metallic *Miscanthus* unpeeling and glinting in the sunshine. We are excited to spot the spiny spider flower again (*Cleome spinosa*) (✽), a cousin of the variety we arranged in Kenya in the autumn.

Harvesting a basketful of flowers, we head back to the narrow green kitchen to arrange them, starting by carefully conditioning each stem. Helen shows me her preferred technique – using a knife – and as I peel, strip and slice she shows me images of Blixen's arrangements and tells me what she has learned of the Baroness's way with flowers.

Blixen lived in partnership with nature; from a young age she loved to be outdoors. An accomplished painter, it was clear that she considered flower arranging a similar medium, another artistic way to express herself. She liked her arrangements to be blowsy, airy and naturalistic, growing many varieties in her garden, cutting but also foraging weeds and wildflowers from the surrounding woods and fields. She tended towards asymmetry and often grouped the visually heaviest flowers at the centre of a display. When guests would come to Rungstedlund to stay she spent the two days beforehand gathering and bringing the outdoors in, often taking into account the character and preferences of her guests. She was greedy when it came to materials, and had the habit of stripping the foliage from her stems so that she could fit more flowers into the vase. On receiving delivery of a florist's bouquet, Blixen would immediately take it apart and reconstruct it to be softer and less rigid but she also loved spiky textures – seed heads and grasses. A competent colourist, she often added splashes of brighter colours to an arrangement so that the contrasting effect would bring the overall palette to life.

Japanese Anemone, Apple and Prince's Feather

Apple (*Malus* – variety unknown)

Black-eyed susan (*Rudbeckia hirta* 'Cappuccino')

Japanese anemone (*Anemone* × *hybrida* 'Robustissima')

Red orache (*Atriplex hortensis* 'Red Plume')

Prince's feather (*Persicaria orientalis*)

Purple fountain grass (*Pennisetum rubrum*)

Porcelain vase from Karen Blixen's collection

The Green Room was one of two that formed Karen Blixen's winter apartment, protected from the chill wind of the Sound that made the other side of the house uninhabitable during the coldest of the winter months. The room is full of memories of Africa – the gramophone given to her by Denys Finch Hatton, the great love of her life, and the cane chair that he loved to sit in beside the fire as she told him her stories. For the arrangement I want to honour the cosy intimacy of this room overlooking the garden, containing some of Karen's most treasured possessions and happiest memories. I choose one of her much loved and often used vases, a porcelain vase edged with gold.

A contemporary of the English floral decorator Constance Spry, Karen Blixen shared a similar fondness for using fruits, vegetables and weeds. Her arrangements celebrated the ephemeral nature of plants when they set seed or decayed, and she happily included withering leaves or the twiggy, skeletal structures of the winter garden. Helen tells me that Blixen liked to create a mass of flowers close to the opening of the vase, inserting the first stems in a neat grid system, allowing the taller stems to splay out in a fan shape. Summer is beginning its dwindling swansong and the Green Room has a sensual melancholy to it. To complement the walls, I choose the pink fireworks of Japanese anemones and toffee *Rudbeckia*. I add windfall apples, the soft wands of ornamental grasses and a wave of the red orache, removing some of the larger leaves and searing the stem ends to prevent the younger stems from wilting.

PREVIOUS
A tranquil, sun-dappled moment at Rungstedlund. Late afternoon, late summer.

OPPOSITE
A fan-shaped floral design incorporating fruits and grasses as Karen Blixen loved to do.

SOLACE IN NATURE
Serge Hill, Hertfordshire, England
September

It is September and the Hertfordshire countryside is a plaid patchwork of gold and green. On a glittering autumn morning we reach the village of Bedmond, turning past the tin church and up to Serge Hill. Here, landscape architect Tom Stuart-Smith and his wife Sue, a psychotherapist and the author of *The Well Gardened-Mind*, have created a community project for gardening, creativity and health. Known as 'The Plant Library' this venture was born from the desire to offer creative therapies harnessing the power of gardening, with the belief that this can radically benefit both mental and physical health. Providing an invaluable educational resource to school children with learning disabilities, mental health charities, horticulture students and gardeners, The Plant Library sits in an old orchard, wrapping around an oak-clad barn known as The Apple House, designed by the couple's son, Benjamin.

Growing, harvesting and creating with a natural material – these are inherently mindful acts. They take us away, out into the fresh

PREVIOUS
The Plant Library at Serge Hill in early autumn.

OPPOSITE
Strong sunshine heightens the contrasts between light and dark, exposure and shade and the drama created by the sparkling inflorescences of the flowers in the wind.

BELOW
The browning bottlebrush flowers of slender-leaved burnet (*Sanguisorba tenuifolia*) dangle above pale lilac asters.

air, our hands in the soil and leaves. The practical labour of tending a garden, conditioning cut flowers, arranging them in a vase – these are methodical, repetitive tasks, but the effects are cathartic and completely natural. Our breathing and heart-rates regulate, pressing anxieties are dampened, to-do lists fade to the back of our minds, thoughts slow and lull. For a short time we are suspended in the here and now, fully in the moment. Most liberating of all is perhaps the reminder that flowers are not in fact, for us. As the reproductive organs of plants, their engaging colours and delicious scents are there to attract pollinators and ensure evolutionary survival of their species. We are simply incredibly lucky to be able to enjoy them. It's a good lesson in how to stop taking things for granted.

Through our work we have had the privilege of connecting with people from all over the world, from many walks and stages of life. While the shared language of plants is universal, each person's way of arranging them is unique and personal. It may be artistic or academic, professional or amateur – the natural offshoot of a gardening vocation, a weekend hobby, a part-time side hustle. For others it is part of an existential quest or a cathartic release. We've welcomed many people to our studio brimming with infectious energy, newly enraptured by the discovery of growing and arranging. A few have been battling

serious illnesses or quietly mourning the loss of someone. Some have been on a spiritual journey, others on a trip creating memories with loved ones, or working through the complex web of emotions as their last child flies the nest and they open a door to a new interest.

Whether you are religious or not, both gardening and flower arranging can be spiritual exercises in acceptance and faith. The ephemerality of plants and cut flowers reminds us of our own mortality. There is also something inherently hopeful about the cyclical nature of life, death and rebirth that we experience in the garden that is particularly beneficial for those grappling with anxiety or depression, coping with trauma or bereavement. Working with the natural world has the power to heal, to comfort, to inspire, to re-energize, to take us to a place of quietude and solace. Flowers force us to slow down and take time. They encourage us to appreciate the beauty in small, everyday moments and in our surrounding landscape. Flowers are able to evoke emotion, to move us, to make us feel surprise, delight, nostalgia. They have a place in moments of celebration and elation, but also in those of grief and sorrow.

ABOVE LEFT
Ripening pears sway in the breeze beside The Apple House.

ABOVE RIGHT
Standing in the Plant Library, a moment of reflection.

OVERLEAF LEFT
The Apple House, Serge Hill, designed by Ben Stuart-Smith.

OVERLEAF RIGHT
Single-variety specimens on display in ceramic bottles and stoneware inkpots.

FINDING FLOWERS
A Library of Plants

The Plant Library is a physical catalogue of over fifteen-hundred varieties of plants that can be walked through, observed and analyzed as they grow. Planted in a grid system across a one-acre site, they are grouped into communities according to their natural preference for conditions: the garden gently sloping from sandy soil and drought-tolerant plants that suit dry, warmer climates at the top; through those preferring more balanced conditions; to damp and shade-loving varieties in moisture-retentive clay soil at the lower end.

Stepping out of The Apple House into the dramatic lighting of an autumn day, it's like arriving at a party to be greeted by a sea of familiar faces and even more interesting-looking strangers – a tiny, freckled toad lily – *Tricyrtis formosana* (✸), a blue, mauve and cream *Viola* 'Janette' (bred by Wildegoose Nursery in Shropshire) (✿), backed by late flowering spires of monkshood (*Aconitum carmichaelii*) (✿), lavender mist meadow rue (*Thalictrum rochebrunianum*) (✸) and oriental hybrid lily (*Lilium speciosum* var. *rubrum* 'Uchina') (✿). Spires of strongly scented baneberry (*Actaea simplex*) are lit up as scudding clouds part overhead and a beam of sparkling sunlight illuminates their bottle brush spikes (✿). Honouring the land's former life as a disused orchard there are pear, apple and damson trees, the latter dropping its fallen fruits into a blue pool of michaelmas daisies (*Aster × frikartii* 'Mönch') (✿). Our attention snags on the deep blue flowers of *Salvia pratensis* 'Giant Form'. Seen through the drying, skeletal forms of *Opopanax chironium* (Hercules's all-heal) (✿), in that moment there is a unique interplay between the two that you can only experience by seeing it first-hand.

As an educational resource, The Plant Library is a clever concept that provides endless inspiration for the garden or floral designer. You can really see how the plants behave, how they interact with one another, and the combinations of form, colour and texture in each grid. The physical experience of following the slope through the varying growing conditions gives a cohesive grasp, in a relatively small space, of what works together, what looks right together. It will be interesting to extrapolate that into a vase.

Bushclover and Asparagus

Aster (*Symphyotrichum* 'Coombe Fishacre')
Garden asparagus (*Asparagus officinalis*)
Ornamental grass (*Panicum elegans* 'Frosted Explosion')
Thunberg's bushclover (*Lespedeza thunbergii*)

Wicker vase
Liner pot

OPPOSITE
In what must have been a case of 'plant blindness', I had never before noticed this exquisite shrub, Thunberg's bushclover, but since our introduction at Serge Hill we seem to keep bumping into one another. Or perhaps it is following me!

I want to make a strong, textural statement for the kitchen counter in The Apple House. Hunting for a graceful branch, one particular shrub – Thunberg's bushclover – calls out to me. Named after the Swedish naturalist Carl Peter Thunberg and a member of the legume family, the leaves are silver-green, interspersed with deep purple flowers. I introduce a pale lilac aster to bridge the two. The centre of their daisy-shaped flowers are turning ginger brown, which conveys a warm, peppery effect.

I line the wicker vase with a suitably sized pot to hold water. As soon as I cut the bushclover I instinctively feel that it will need searing – the leaves begin to droop almost immediately. I dip the stem ends in boiling water for a few seconds. A stream of bubbles pours out and this works the magic trick of removing the air block, shooting water up through the capillaries of the woody stems. Within minutes they are perky and dancing again. I want these stems to cascade and do their fountain-like thing without any focal flowers to detract from their slender, arching shapes. The addition of asparagus, aster and the plume-like switch grass assume the roles of misty support-acts but the bushclover is the star of the show.

'Experiencing beauty has been found to be accompanied by neural activation in regions of our brain which play a vital role in integrating our thoughts, feelings and motivations and damping down our fear and stress responses. Beauty calms and revitalizes us – it is an essential ingredient of life.'
SUE STUART-SMITH

Liquorice, Asters and Oats

Aster (*Aster glehnii* 'Agleni')

Baneberry (*Actaea simplex* 'Mountain Wave', 'Pink Spike' and 'White Pearl')

Golden oats (*Stipa gigantea*)

Japanese anemone (*Anemone* × *hybrida* 'Loreley')

Sweet coneflower (*Rudbeckia subtomentosa* 'Little Henry')

Tall buckwheat (*Fagopyrum dibotrys*)

Yunnan liquorice (*Glycyrrhiza yunnanensis*)

Terracotta jar

The Apple House is an open-plan barn that finds a perfect synergy between modern and rustic. The building materials are natural, all sourced within a ten-mile radius – the flooring is unfired clay tiles, the cladding oak, the walls hempcrete. I choose this tall terracotta vase to draw the eye to the far corner of the room and the magnificent view of the garden beyond. The proportions of the room seem to demand height. As the weather worsens throughout the day, the interiors dim and call for lightness.

There are certain plants in certain places that you remember and revisiting them feels like seeing an old friend. We annually seek out a Yunnan liquorice at Chelsea Physic Garden in London – in winter the bristly seedheads are golden brown, standing tall well into winter. I choose these to use as my branches because they are suitably statuesque but the leaves still elegant. Criss-crossing the stalks inside the jar creates the first in a network of supporting stems. The buckwheat and baneberry tick the height and white boxes, with a few yellow coneflowers and the beaten gold shimmer of *Stipa* grasses. I cut a few of the lacy bronze baneberry leaves and tuck them in around the neck of the vase as a collar. The flower spikelets are extraordinary; I use some of the pure white and a pair tinged with purple that picks up on the reddish seedheads of the liquorice. To salute the barn as a place of community and horticultural learning, I place the pair so that they meet in the middle, as if in conversation or embrace.

OPPOSITE
A naturalistic arrangement created mindfully and slowly, taking cues from these tall, graceful ingredients and placing them where they naturally wish to go.

THE WILD WEST
Aberglasney, Carmarthenshire
& Dyffryn Fernant, Pembrokeshire, Wales
October

It's headlong into autumn now and we're heading as far west as we can go before we hit the sea. Wide skies and open country beckon. The roads narrow hour by hour, greyly threading through a thick tapestry of green and gold. The landscape changes in increments – urban to provincial, rural to hinterland, and then wild. Deep into the Black Mountains, we take a meandering detour along the river to Nant-y-Bedd. An organic garden we've long wanted to visit, the name translates from the Welsh for 'stream of the grave', which trickles down from the Bronze Age burial mounds up on the mountain. The gardens blur into thick conifer forest and feel not so much 'in' the woods as part of them. We're led into the potager by Sue, who has been lovingly tending the garden for over forty years, and into a beautifully chaotic tangle of perennial vegetables and self-sown weeds permitted to find their own place among them. Sue is passionate about the value of many of these often-dismissed plants and is generous with her knowledge of the beneficial roles they play medicinally, for pollinators, and as delicious and nutritious edibles. Her aesthetic is finding beauty in the transience and imperfections of nature – an outpost of the *wabi sabi* philosophy in the Welsh mountains.

After stopping to admire the flowering chicory and a particularly majestic 'Taunton Deane' kale plant, we venture across a swaying rope bridge and find a natural swimming pond overlooking sloping woodland pasture. Here, we veer around and along the bank of the Grwyne Fawr river under a thick canopy of colossal pines before climbing back into the woods and looping over the road in a figure of eight to survey the view back down the hill. We explore the edible forest garden and the cottage garden and bury ourselves nosily in the greenhouse, which is thick with vines, the last rays of slanting sunlight transpose the leaves a smoky red in the underglow. As we say our goodbyes we stop to appreciate a bountifully berried *Leycesteria formosa* (which has a slew of wonderful common names including

PREVIOUS
Jess photographing an arrangement of sword, spire and trumpet shapes from the enchanting garden of Dyffryn Fernant, Pembrokeshire.

OPPOSITE
The leaves of a grape vine lit by mellow autumn sunlight in the greenhouse of Sue and Ian Mabberley at Nant-y-Bedd in the Brecon Beacons.

ABOVE LEFT
Sundried grasses and umbels.

ABOVE RIGHT
The natural swimming pond at Nant-y-Bedd.

pheasant bush, chocolate berry, partridge berry, flowering nutmeg and Himalayan honeysuckle). The fruits are plump, delicious and taste of burnt caramel.

Across the Brecon Beacons and into the hilly uplands of Carmarthenshire. Known as 'the garden of Wales', this is surely one of the most beautiful counties in the UK. In the Towy Valley is Aberglasney, a primrose yellow mansion encircled by twenty different styles of garden over ten acres. On a small hill behind the house an Asiatic area is planted with rare trees and shrubs from China, Japan and Nepal, and an Alpinum of diminutive dwarf plants that is exquisite in the spring when the hill becomes a watercolour of ice blue, pale yellow and rust. In the mansion an indoor Ninfarium houses a collection of subtropical and exotic plants. Directly below the building an Elizabethan cloister garden encloses the central lawn with a solid stone arcaded walkway dating to the 1600s. The gardens seem to go on and on as you follow the hill-slope – a formal walled garden designed by Penelope Hobhouse leads into a productive kitchen garden of step-over fruit trees and vegetables planted in a strategic crop rotation with flowers for cutting. Below, a hundred-metre-long (328-ft) wall is planted with a collection of over thirty different varieties of rambling rose, and a meadowy stream garden runs into ferny woodland – my

favourite area in the spring when thousands of *Narcissi bulbocodium* (hoop petticoat daffodil) and *Fritillaria meleagris* (Snake's head fritillary) shiver in the breeze.

I first came to Aberglasney one summer day over ten years ago in the first flush of my love affair with flowers. I remember standing in the Lower Walled Garden beneath a bewitching tunnel of crab apple (*Malus sargentii*) and being aware that a new world had opened up to me – a world of plants and flowers and gardens – and it was as if I had never noticed them before, or I was seeing the world through fresh eyes and suddenly every inch, from meadow to motorway verge, was alive with magic and possibility. I was thirty years old and for the previous decade had been living the life of a drifter, settling briefly in different places and jobs and then feeling restless and moving on. I had no real plan for what I wanted to do, only the vaguely persistent feeling that at some point, it would find me. The garden here was where that finally came to pass and so it has remained something of a sentimental touchstone. Every year I make the pilgrimage to revisit and take stock and every year I've loved stretching my eyes across this view and seeing it through that same prism of emotions, which seem to deepen and expand and yet are somehow also circuitous, like an Escher staircase. Bringing Jess here for the first time felt like coming full circle.

ABOVE LEFT
We're accompanied by curious robins everywhere we go. A particularly fine specimen at Nant-y-Bedd.

ABOVE RIGHT
The Walled Garden at Aberglasney, designed by Penelope Hobhouse.

FINDING FLOWERS
Low-hanging Fruit

Today the gardens are redolent of approaching autumn. The roseate orbs of apples are being gathered by the hundreds along the latticed Belgian fence – an astonishing twenty-five-metre (82-ft) espalier flanking the Upper Walled Garden. Within, the borders are awash with smoky pink and mauves caught by burnished tints of gold and copper. Dahlias drift into Joe Pye weed (*Eupatorium purpureum*), *Phlox paniculata*, catmint (*Nepeta*), monkshood (*Aconitum*), geranium 'Rozanne' (✽), *Stipa gigantea*, the soft yellow *Helianthus* 'Lemon Queen' and pure white *Anemone* × *hybrida* 'Honorine Jobert'. Throughout the garden the trees are in full regalia now, occasional branches draped with subtle green lichen. There are Japanese maples, Tupelo (*Nyssa sylvatica*), witch hazel (*Hamamelis*), red oak (*Quercus rubra*), sweet gum (*Liquidambar styraciflua*) and pin oak (*Quercus palustris*). Pools of colour beneath make for mouth-watering tableaus, the sugary tempered with dashes of the acidic – citrine and lime, and milk-white lilies (✽). The entrance to the glass Melon House is strung with a radiantly fiery bunting of Virginia Creeper (*Parthenocissus quinquefolia*).

There are treasures to discover around every corner but we're drawn back to the fruitiness of the kitchen garden and the hushed tranquility of the woodland. Here, puddles of ivy-leaved *Cyclamen* (✽) and autumn crocus (*Colchicum autumnale*) are spot-lit by slants of sunlight in the dim shade of tall pines, a clump of hardy begonia is illuminated (*Begonia grandis* subsp. 'Evansiana') (✽), the underbelly of its waxy olive-green leaves a map of fine red veins. We spot a late-flowering *Clematis* 'Praecox' (✽), the woody scrambling stems smothered with white stars that are tipped with grey-blue. This is where the hydrangea are and they are in their prime – vast clouds of mopheads, mountain and oak leaf varieties with papery, speckled corymbs in powder blue, shell pink and raspberry. The exquisite *Hydrangea aspera* 'Hot Chocolate' combines soft brown leaves with wine-red undersides and intricate lace-cap, two-tone flowers.

Willowherb and Coral Bark Maple

Apple (*Malus domestica* 'Brith Mawr',
   Malus domestica 'Pig Aderyn')
Clematis 'Praecox'
Coral bark maple (*Acer palmatum* 'Sango-kaku')
Hairy willowherb (*Epilobium hirsutum*)
French hydrangea (*Hydrangea macrophylla*)
Japanese lily (*Lilium speciosum* 'Album')
Japanese wisteria (*Wisteria floribunda*
   'Yae-Kokuryū')
Mandarin rose (*Rosa moyesii*)
Masterwort (*Astrantia maxima*)
Mountain hydrangea (*Hydrangea serrata*)
Oak leaved hydrangea (*Hydrangea quercifolia*)
Panicled hydrangea (*Hydrangea paniculata*
   'Vanilla Fraise')
Rough-leaved hydrangea (*Hydrangea aspera*)
Smooth hydrangea (*Hydrangea arborescens*
   'Pink Annabelle')
Solomon's seal (*Polygantum × hybridum*)
Spindle (*Euonymus europaeus*)

Cast iron urn
Kenzan
Chicken wire

OPPOSITE
A flickering, smoky arrangement to celebrate the October apple harvest at Aberglasney.

Of any season, autumn is the one in which to embrace and experiment with texture. Walking the gardens we are struck by the wispy plumes of willowherb rising like pale smoke from the borders where it has self-seeded. We decide to set up in one of the arched cloisters that has a shadowy, monastic atmosphere; the ancient stone walls give us an interesting textural backdrop to arrange against. I blag the apples from the gardeners who generously bring crates of their abundant harvest. They add a beautiful warm green to the scene and complement the fading ovate leaves of the Solomon's seal.

I use a rusted cast-iron garden urn, which suits the cloistered setting. Taking time to wrangle the tall branches into place, I split the woodier stems and push them firmly onto a large pinholder in the base to ensure they are secure. I concentrate the shorter stems of multi-coloured foliage around the base of the vessel, adding whiskery whips of Japanese wisteria and rose to create a bold asymmetric outline, layering the hydrangea and the tousled tangle of willowherb in a low 'U' shape to draw the eye towards the solitary milky lily at the centre. In the murk of the autumn afternoon, the richer colours are tempted to recede into the darkness so I gather an equal quantity of pale material. The white is essentially lifting – visually it advances and pulls the smoky red and orange forwards out of the shadows.

See, below, the pleasant dome,
The poet's pride, the poet's home....
See her woods, where Echo talks,
Her gardens trim, her terrace walks,
Her wildernesses, fragrant brakes,
Her gloomy bowers and shining lakes,
Keep, ye gods, this humble seat,
For ever pleasant, private, neat.

From 'The Country Walk' by John Dyer (1699–1757).
The painter and landscape poet was raised at Aberglasney.

FINDING FLOWERS
The Last Stop

From Carmarthen we keep driving until we can see the sea, which takes a while because for much of the way there is congestion (sheep in the road). Dyffryn Fernant is midway between Newport and Fishguard on the Pembrokeshire coast. We arrive after dark – and in Pembrokeshire, this is very, very dark – fumble our way to the Bothy and into bed. In the morning, we open the latch door and step into a Welsh Eden.

Christina Shand takes us up the grassy slope behind the house to the Magic Garden, a viewing mound bounded by the witchy, windswept shapes of hawthorn. From here you can get your bearings and an idea of the position of the garden as a whole. The six-acre site faces east and runs down a steep hill that is half rock, half bog, with a wild marsh and the Fernant stream at the bottom. The house – painted the colour of raspberry fool – is south-facing, unusual for Pembrokeshire, and Christina tells us that she made a conscious choice not to have boundaries around the garden, intending the periphery to melt into the surrounding landscape.

Previously home to a small family farm with a herd of milking cattle, Christina bought Dyffryn Fernant in 1994, tentatively beginning to garden the overgrown farmyard two years later. Focusing first on the rampageous brambles, bracken, blackthorn and Japanese knotweed she laid out the Front Garden with a local friend – raised beds and pots of dahlias, *Salvia* and mallow are encircled by a stone wall (✺). The Kitchen Garden, behind the house, followed with four course crop rotation for vegetables as well as culinary herbs. Slowly, over many years, the rest of the garden was built and planted according to each area's specific soil conditions, which ranges from acidic to neutral loam over blue clay.

We venture down to the Bog Garden past a peeling Persian ironwood tree (*Parrotia persica*) (✺). Christina refers to this as the 'lung' of the garden. Here the wild and cultivated collide; it is lush and oozy, teeming with pre-historic plants and monstrously large leaves – *Gunnera manicata*, the sword-like New Zealand flax (*Phormium*) and silver spear (*Astelia*), bulrush (*Typha latifolia*), Indian elecampane (*Inula racemosa*) and common reed (*Phragmites australis*) – in the 'rhôs pasture' beyond stand spires of water figwort (*Scrophularia auriculata*) (✺). A stainless steel obelisk refracts the light and reflects the rustling leaves. In Hopeful Wood a group of trees, including walnut, red oak (*Quercus rubra*), pocket handkerchief tree (*Davidia involucrata*), tulip tree (*Liriodendron tulipifera*) and apple (*Malus*), stand watch. We make a note to return in the spring when the ground beneath is carpeted with *Narcissi*, *Camassia* and early purple orchid (*Orchis mascula*).

Dyffryn Fernant has a spiritual atmosphere. Looking to the horizon, the rocky outcrop of Garn Fawr crowns the Preseli Hills (✷) where the Stonehenge bluestones came from over five thousand years ago. This is an intensely emotional and personal garden, too. Christina notices everything – a butterfly fluttering through branches of a swamp oak, the scent of cinder toffee from a *Katsura* tree, the wind-burnt leaves on a wild cherry in the Kitchen Garden. In 'Nikki's Field' (✽) around a central oak tree she has planted a checkerboard grid of thirty square beds, each exhibiting a different species of grass or sedge in memory of her brother, Nicholas. It is a simple but beautifully effective concept, a peaceful place to sit and listen to the shiver and swish of the stems. Across the pond, David's Wood was planted by Christina's husband in 2003; birch trees rise from a swamp of reflections.

Reaching the very bottom of the slope we come to The Beyond. The Fernant stream carves its wriggly way through and here the conditions are polar opposite to where we started up in the Magic Garden. We turn our backs to the lichen and old willows to complete our circular walk of the plot through an ancient rush pasture of meadowsweet, valerian, wild angelica and scabious. Up into the Orchard, where a linear path divides mixed borders of grasses, herbaceous perennials and fruit trees and guides us towards a dawn redwood tree (*Metasequoia glyptostroboides*) (✽) at the far end with feathered leaves on their way to a foxy brown. In the Rickyard an old oil jar positioned under a rusted frame is surrounded by formal topiary of box, pittosporum and yew, and beds of intersectional peonies and *Agapanthus*. On past the Library and we find ourselves back at the centre of the garden, with a full page of scribbled names and a very long 'shopping list' for arrangements.

This garden is so layered with alluring nooks and niches, and exotic, unusual varieties that I am as daunted by the sheer choice as I was at Dixter in July. There is an extraordinary range of plants we have never come across before – Chinese rice paper plant (*Tetrapanax papyrifer* 'Rex'), *Acer palmatum* 'Koto-no-eto', *Salvia* 'Phyllis's Fancy' and *Cornus* 'Venus'. Perhaps it is this tentative excitement that influences what I choose and the way I cut – taking just one or two single stems, but from a wide range of varieties. I'm magnetically drawn to the flashes of red in the Orchard – crimson flag lilies (*Hesperantha coccinea*) (✽) and sabra spike sage (*Salvia confertiflora*) (✽) – and the vibrant pinks in front of the farmhouse. I'm curious to explore the tension in subduing these with earthy bronze tones. Setting out with bucket and snips, a colour story develops as I walk.

Meadowsweet and Marsh Mallow

Bulrush (*Typha latifolia*)

Loosestrife (*Lythrum salicaria*)

Marsh mallow (*Althaea officinalis*)

Primrose (*Primula veris*)

Queen of the prairie (*Filipendula rubra* 'Venusta')

Royal fern (*Osmunda regalis*)

Variegated common reed (*Phragmites australis* subsp. *australis* 'Variegatus')

Jug by Sally Seymour

Darling, could you bring me some flowers back from the bog? Perhaps not the most poetic request. It is an interesting exercise to take a particular area of a garden – a border, a rose or kitchen garden – and make something just from that specific environment. At least you know the plants will look right together, because they are living proof they will happily share the same soil conditions, position and season. While there are uncomfortable truths about a dahlia sharing a vase with a peony or a tulip, a marriage of bulrush and marsh mallow, now that's another story...

In this naturalistic arrangement, form and texture come to the fore over colour – the interest is in the tension and contrast these varying materials make together in a grouping. A slice of the most intriguing part of the garden at Dyffryn Fernant, it is a slender cutaway of this very specific and unique collection of plants from the outer bog – feathery metallic rushes, spires of loosestrife, the chocolate seedhead of a bulrush, meadowsweet gone to seed. In midsummer, this would be candy-floss pink but has faded now to a crisp russet. I arrange them in no particular order, grouping the hairy leaves of the primrose to create a focal area bottom right.

PREVIOUS LEFT
Pink montbretia (*Tritonia disticha* subsp. *rubrolucens*).

PREVIOUS RIGHT
An arrangement using the autumn bounty of a true visionary plantswoman, Christina Shand, owner and creator of the garden at Dyffryn Fernant.

OPPOSITE
Celebrating the humble and overlooked.

Red Dragon

Autumn sage (*Salvia greggii* 'Royal Bumble')
Beard tongue (*Penstemon* 'Garnet')
Bridal wreath (*Francoa sonchifolia*)
Flag lily (*Hesperantha coccinea*)
Guernsey lily (*Nerine bowdenii* 'Mr John')
Japanese lace fern (*Polystichum polyblepharum*)
Mallow (a gift – variety unknown)
Pink montbretia (*Tritonia disticha* subsp. *rubrolucens*)
Sabra spike sage (*Salvia confertiflora*)
Small-headed knotweed (*Persicaria microcephala* 'Red Dragon')
Strawberry (*Fragaria* × *ananassa*)
Yellow loosestrife (*Lysimachia ciliata* 'Firecracker')

French ceramic pot with stoneware glaze
Chicken wire

Christina kneels beside the Aga, riffling through a cupboard in search of vases. She pulls out a few ceramics including this large French pot. From my garden harvest I have in mind a lustrous, fruity display of jewel-like pink and reds against brown-toned foliage. The rich honey glaze of the pot complements this nicely and adds a rustic grounding to the composition.

We're deep in fern country here and the feathery leaves are ideal for fanning out as a foliage base. First I fit a small dome of chicken wire inside the vase for stability – I've cut a lot of spindly stemmed materials and they need support. The earthy bronze of the bistort is a good compromise against the brash pink of the nerines and seems to keep them in check. I stagger the mallow and dried bridal wreath stems in an upwards sweep and allow the montbretia to gesture wildly at them from the opposite side. The awkward shapes and angles of these stems are jarring but I think that's what makes the whole arrangement seem spirited and appear to be dancing as the sun sets. It is, after all, a celebration of the garden, and of being here to see it.

OPPOSITE
'Shall we dance?' the Tritonia seem to say. I let them lead the way.

Directory

ABERGLASNEY GARDENS
Llangathen, Carmarthen, Wales, SA32 8QH
www.aberglasney.org • @aberglasney

BARBARA HEPWORTH MUSEUM
AND SCULPTURE GARDEN
Barnoon Hill, Saint Ives, TR26 1AD
www.tate.org.uk • @tatestives

CARA GUTHRIE CERAMICS
www.caraguthrieceramics.com
@caraguthrieceramics

CHARLESTON
Firle, West Firle, Lewes, BN8 6LL
www.charleston.org.uk • @charlestontrust

DYFFRYN FERNANT GARDEN
Fishguard, Pembrokeshire, Wales, SA65 9SP
www.dyffrynfernant.co.uk • @dyffryn_fernant_garden

ECOSCAPES
Moi North Lake Road, Naivasha, Kenya
www.ecoscapes.co.ke • @ecoscapeskenya

ELLIOTT'S
21 Sciennes Rd, Edinburgh, Scotland, EH9 1NX
www.elliottsedinburgh.com • @jess_elliott_dennison

GREAT DIXTER HOUSE AND GARDENS
Northiam, Rye, East Sussex, TN31 6PH
www.greatdixter.co.uk • @greatdixterofficial

HADITHI HQ
Kasigau Road, Maungu, Kenya
www.hadithikenya.com • @hadithi_crafts

KAREN BLIXEN MUSEUM RUNGSTEDLUND
Rungsted Strandvej 111, 2960 Rungsted Kyst, Denmark
www.blixen.dk • @karenblixenrungstedlund

LES TERRES DE PIERRE
Hameau de Baumettes, 13890, Mouriès, France
www.lesterresdepierre.com
@lesterresdepierre • @pruneplumes

MADE IN CLEY
Starr House, High Street, Holt, NR25 7RF
www.madeincley.co.uk • @made_in_cley

NANT-Y-BEDD GARDEN
Fforest Coal Pit, Abergavenny, Wales, NP7 7LY
www.nantybedd.com • @nantybeddgarden

POTERIE RAVEL
8 Av. des Goums, 13400 Aubagne, France
www.poterie-ravel.com • @poterieravel

PYRUS BOTANICALS
Walled Garden, West Saltoun, Pencaitland, EH34 5DS
www.pyrusbotanicals.com • @pyrusbotanicals

SISSINGHURST CASTLE GARDEN
Biddenden Rd, Cranbrook, TN17 2AB
www.nationaltrust.org.uk

THE COASTAL EXPLORATION COMPANY
Wells-Next-the-Sea, North Norfolk
www.coastalexplorationcompany.co.uk
@coastalexplorationcompany

THE LEACH POTTERY
Higher Stennack, Saint Ives, TR26 2HE
www.leachpottery.com • @theleachpottery

THE OPPORTUNITY FACTORY
Mbagathi Ridge, Nairobi, Kenya
www.opportunityfactory.co • @opportunityfactory

THE SERGE HILL PROJECT
The Orchard, Featherbed Ln, Abbots Langley, WD5 0RZ
www.sergehillproject.co.uk • @sergehillproject

THE SHELL MUSEUM
Church House, Hurdle Ln, Glandford, Holt, NR25 7JR
www.shellmuseum.org.uk • @glandfordshellmuseum

TRINITY COTTAGE
202 High St, Aldeburgh, IP15 5AJ, UK
@trinitycottagesuffolk • @kristinperers

TURN END HOUSE AND GARDEN
9 Townside, Haddenham, Aylesbury, HP17 8BG
www.turnend.org.uk • @turnendtrust

WIVETON HALL
Wiveton, Holt, NR25 7TE
www.wivetonhall.co.uk • @wivetonhall

Acknowledgments

The making of this book has involved a great many people who have generously given of their time to help, support and host us, for which we are very grateful. Our heartfelt thanks go to:

Our editor Fleur Jones at Thames & Hudson for commissioning this book and putting your trust in us from the beginning. Kristin Perers for being an inspiration to us both in so many ways, for the portrait and the chance to spend time by the sea in your pink cottage talking through ideas for this book. It all started there. Sarah and Tony Seth-Smith for welcoming old friends back to your magical corner of Lake Naivasha, for the landcruiser lifts and the whiskey. Alex and Richard Bell for a memorable few days at Ecoscapes, letting us gather from the farm and for hosting a fabulous workshop and lunch. Troy Scott-Smith, Saffron Prentis and John Sutherland at Sissinghurst Castle Garden. Tressa Lapham-Green at the Barbara Hepworth Museum and Matt Tyas at Leach Pottery for your collaboration and kindness (and our Jason-Statham-lookalike taxi driver in St Ives for carting us and our buckets around). Peter and Margaret Aldington; Turn End is a uniquely special place that unfailingly offers insight and motivation. Jackie Hunt – thank you for your thoughtful notes, for the detail of your plant knowledge, for the most exquisite rose canes and for the Jaffa Cakes. William and Prune Revoil; thank you for everything: the food, the wine, the olive oil, the flowers, the laughs and cuddles with Rosalie. Fergus Garrett and the team for the extraordinary garden that is Great Dixter. Coralie Thomas for answering our endless WhatsApp queries and Daniel James for your kind introductions. The Charleston Trust, Cathy Crisp and Harry Hoblyn for a happy day arranging in the farmhouse and for the use of Quentin Bell's vases. Heidi Francis for telling us about the owls hooting in the dusk on Holkham Beach (and many other wonderful suggestions and introductions over the years). Henry Chamberlain and Nick Stokes at Coastal Exploration Co for your local knowledge, kindness and delicious pork pies. Desmond MacCarthy for the hilarity of your company and allowing us to borrow from Chloe's vase collection. Amanda Bennett at Wiveton for your time and insights. Made in Cley pottery for the loan of your divine ceramics and for providing many of our favourite pieces over the years. The Shell Museum, Glandford for accommodating us at short notice and Susie in the cottage opposite ours for the hydrangea swag. Jess Elliott Dennison at Elliott's, Edinburgh who we so admire. Thank you for feeding us and inspiring us on a regular basis, you are a true powerhouse. Fiona Inglis at Pyrus Botanicals for sharing your beautiful garden and all the treasures you grow, for the strawberries and coffee and for the lift. Christina Kaas at the Karen Blixen Museum for your enthusiasm and encouragement and Helen Olsen for sharing your knowledge of Karen Blixen's flower arranging practice; our day learning from you was one we will cherish. Tom and Sue Stuart-Smith for the extraordinary gift that is The Plant Library at Serge Hill and to Millie Souter and Rebecca Finch for welcoming us so kindly. Sue and Ian Mabberley for letting us explore the spellbinding Nant-y-Bedd and nibble on toffee-flavoured pheasant berries. Dave Hand and the team at Aberglasney; the garden where it all began. Thank you for the copious delivery of apples throughout the day and for nurturing a place that brings joy and solace. Christina and David Shand at Dyffryn Fernant; what an extraordinarily personal and spiritual place you have created. Thank you for your hospitality and warmth; we will be back. Sarah Caffyn for your nurturing friendship and the rare tranquillity of your Sussex garden. To Mum and Dad, Ed and Ben, thank you for the colossal amount of love and support you give us, and to Guy and Agnes, thank you for being the two sweetest flowers to come home to.

Authors' Biography

AESME STUDIO was founded in 2015 by sisters Jess and Alex. We are passionate about sharing the meditative process of arranging flowers, the transformative power of plants and the joy they bring.

Our main studio is a converted railway arch in Shepherd's Bush, London where we design for events, teach workshops and make films. We grow flowers in a small garden in Hampshire, specializing in naturalistic floral design with a strong focus on using seasonal materials and sustainable techniques.

Website   aesme.co.uk
Films   flowersonfilm.aesme.co.uk
Instagram & YouTube   @aesmestudio

ABOVE
Jess (left) and Ally (right).

Index

Page references in *italics* refer to illustrations.

A

Aberglasney, Carmarthen 217-23
Acacia 50, 51
aesthetics 13
African lily (*Agapanthus*) 60, 61, *164*
African rosemallow (*Hibiscus acetosella*) *12*, *62*, *63*
African starbush (*Grewia occidentalis*) 50, 51, *54*, *55*
Aldeburgh, England 21-29
Aldington, Peter and Margaret 89
alexanders (*Smyrnium*)
  alexanders (*S. olusatrum*) 71, *76*, *77*
  perfoliate (*S. perfoliatum*) 122, *123*, *126*, *127*
Alliums 108, *109*, 182, *183*
Aloe vera 51
amaranth 182, *183*
Anemone
  Balkan (*A. blanda*) 6
  Japanese (*A.* × *hybrida*) 33, 152, *153*, *194*, *195*, *198*, *199*, 212, *213*
  windflower (*A. coronaria* 'The Bride') *82*, *83*
angel's fishing rod (*Dierama pulcherimum*) 115, 118, *119*, 122, *123*, *126*, *127*
apple (*Malus*) 80, *81*, 182, *183*, *198*, *199*, 222, *223*
Arabian pea (*Bituminaria bituminosa*) 108, *109*
art 135
asparagus *106*, *107*, 210, 211
aster (*Aster glehnii* 'Agleni') 212, *213*
aster (*Symphyotrichum*) 210, 211

B

baby's breath (*Gypsophila elegans* 'Convent Garden') *184*, *185*
bamboo (*Bambusa*) *124*, *125*
baneberry (*Actaea simplex* 'Mountain Wave', 'Pink Spike' and 'White Pearl') 209, 212, *213*
Barbados gooseberry (*Pereskia aculeata*) *56*, *57*
bay (*Laurus nobilis*) 37
beard tongue (*Penstemon* 'Garnet') 232, *233*
bear's breeches (*Acanthus mollis*) *118*, *119*
beauty bower (*Pandorea jasminoides*) *56*, *57*
Begonia 220, *221*
Bell, Alex 61
Bell, Quentin 131, 139
Bell, Vanessa 131-32, 135, 143
bellflowers (*Campanula*)
  milky (*C. lactiflora*) *126*, *127*
  rampion (*C. rapunculus*) 118, 119
black-eyed susan (*Rudbeckia hirta*) *198*, *199*
blackberries 180, 181, 182, *183*
Bladder campion (*Silene vulgaris*) 108, *109*
Bladder senna (*Colutea orientalis*) *162*, *163*
Blixen, Karen 48, 189-90, 195, 199
Bloomsbury Group 131-32
Bougainvillea 46, 49, 50, 51, *56*, *57*
Box (*Buxus sempervirens*) 37
Bracken (*Pteridium aquilinum*) 22, 27, 152, *153*
Bridal wreath (*Francoa sonchifolia*) 232, *233*
Buckwheat (*Fagopyrum dibotrys*) 212, *213*
Bulrush (*Typha latifolia*) *230*, *231*
Burnet (*Sanguisorba tenuifolia* var. *Alba*) *126*, *127*
Buttercup (*Ranunculus repens*) *124*, *125*

C

Calendula officinalis 180, 181, 182, *183*
California tree poppy (*Romneya coulteri*) 157, *164*, *165*
Camellia japonica 69, 80, *81*
Cape leadwort (*Plumbago auriculata*) *54*, *55*
Centaury (*Centaurium littorale*) *148*, *149*
Chain fern (*Woodwardia*) *230*, *231*
Charleston Farmhouse, East Sussex, England 128-30, 131-43
Cherry trees
  Himalayan (*Prunus cerasoides* 'Puddum') 50, 51, *54*, *55*
  Prunus 'Accolade' 66, *80*, *81*
  Winter flowering (*Prunus* × *subhirtella* 'Autumnalis') 36, 37, *42*, *43*
Chilean iris (*Libertia ixioides*) *76*, *77*
China aster (*Callistephus chinensis* 'King Size Apricot') 180, 181, *184*, *185*
Christmas 37, 41-42, 48
Chrysanthemum 42, *43*
Clematis 37, 220, *221*, 222, *223*
Cleome gynandra 60, 61
Cleome spinosa *194*, *195*
Cocksfoot (*Dactylis glomerata*) 108, *109*
Coneflowers, sweet (*Rudbeckia subtomentosa* 'Little Henry') 212, *213*
Containers, choosing 85
Coral bells (*Heuchera* 'Marmalade') 80, *81*, *84*, *85*
Corncockle (*Agrostemma githago* 'Light Rose') *142*, *143*
Cornelian cherry (*Cornus mas*) 36, 37
Cornflowers (*Centaurea cyanus*) 118, *119*, 122, *123*, 135, *138*, *139*, 180, 181
Cornwall, England 64-66, 67-85
Cranesbill (*Geranium pratense*) 122, *123*, *162*, *163*
Creeping thistle (*Cirsium arvense*) *176*, *177*
Crocosmia 115, *126*, *127*
Crocuses 38, *39*
Culpeper, Nicholas 181
Curry plant (*Helichrysum italicum*) *140*, *141*, *142*, *143*
Cyclamen 25, *26*, *27*, 220, *221*

D

Daffodils (*Narcissus*) 80, *81*, *82*, *83*
Dahlias 33
Dawn redwood tree (*Metasequoia glyptostroboides*) 226, *227*
Daylily (*Hemerocallis* 'Corky') 122, *123*, *160*, *161*
Dyer, John 223

Dyffryn Fernant, Pembrokeshire 214-15, 224, 225-32

E

East Sussex, England 11, 110-12, 113-27, 128-30, 131-43
Ecoscapes market garden 59-60, 61
Edible arrangements 182, *183*
Edinburgh, Scotland 166-68, 169-85
Elliott Dennison, Jess 169-70
Epimedium 38
Eucalyptus stuartiana 80, *81*
Evening primrose (*Oenothera glazioviana*) 118, *119*, 122, *123*, 157

F

Fairy wings (*Epimedium* × *warleyense* 'Orangekönigin') *84*, *85*
Farewell to spring (*Clarkia amoena*) *126*, *127*
Fennel (*Foeniculum vulgare*) 12, 26, 27, 28, *29*, *62*, *63*
Ferns (*Dryopteris* and *Pteridophyta*) 122, *123*, 232, *233*
Flag lilies (*Hesperantha coccinea*) 226, *227*, 232, *233*
Flag lily (*Hesperantha coccinea*) 232, *233*
Foam flower (*Tiarella cordifolia*) *82*, *83*
Food 169-73, 182
Foster, Matt 85
Fox-and-cubs (*Pilosella aurantiaca*) *162*, *163*
Foxglove beardtongue (*Penstemon*) *164*, *165*
Foxglove (*Digitalis*) 135, 140, *141*, 157, *173*, 180, 181, *184*, *185*
Frangipani 47, 51
Fringe cup (*Tellima grandiflora*) *82*, *83*
Fritillaria
  F. verticillata 38, *39*
  'Green Dreams' 64-65, 80, *81*
  Pointed-petal fritillary (*F. acmopetala*) *82*, *83*
  Seedheads *92*, *93*
  Snakeshead fritillary (*F. meleagris*) *82*, *83*
Fry, Roger 132, 143
Fuchsia 156, 157, *164*, *165*

G

Garlic 82, *83*, 182, *183*
Garnett, David 'Bunny' 135, 139
Garrett, Fergus 114
Geraniums 220, 221 *see also* cranesbill
Grant, Duncan 131-32, 135, 140
Grasses 27
    Natal grass (*Melinis repens*) 56, *57*, 62, *63*
    Ornamental grass (*Panicum elegans* 'Roseum') *198*, 199, 210, 211, 212, *213*
Great Dixter, East Sussex, England 11, 110-12, *113-27*
Great millet (*Sorghum*) 62, *63*
Great mullein (*Verbascum thapsus*) 42, *43*
Guernsey lily (*Nerine bowdenii* 'Mr John') 232, *233*

H

Hairy chervil (*Chaerophyllum hirsutum* 'Roseum') 122, *123*
Hairy willowherb (*Epilobium hirsutum*) 222, *223*
Heaths 18-19, 21-22
Hedge bedstraw (*Gallium mollugo*) 126, *127*
Hepworth, Barbara 67-68, 71, 82
Hercules's all-heal (*Opopanax chironium*) 208, *209*
Hertfordshire, England 200-202, *203-13*
Hesiod 28
Hibiscus 12, 62, *63*
Hobhouse, Penelope 217
Holly (*Ilex aquifolium*) 37
Hollyhocks (*Alcea rosea*) *134*, 135, *148*, 149, *158-60*
Honesty (*Lunaria annua*) 37, 114
Honeysuckle (*Lonicera*) 92, *93*, 102, *103*, *138*, 139, 152, *153*
Hops (*Humulus lupulus*) 182, *183*
Hornbeam (*Carpinus betulus*) 37
Hunt, Jackie 93
Hydrangea 126, *127*, *148*, 149, 152, *153*, *188*, 221, 222, *223*

I

Inglis, Fiona *174-75*, 177
Installation arrangements *30-31*, 33
Iris, bearded iris (*I. germanica*) 92, *93*, *94*, *95*

J

Jacaranda 54, *55*
Jammy mouth (*Ruttya fruticosa*) 56, *57*
Japanese snow flower (*Deutzia × elegantissima* 'Rosealind'). 91, *94*, *95*
Japanese spindle (*Euonymus japonicus*) 76, *77*
Jekyll, Gertrude 132
Jerusalem sage (*Phlomis fruticosa*) 108, *109*
Jodrell, Alfred 152

K

Kent, England 6, 30-32, *33-43*
Kenya, East Africa 12, 44-46, *47-63*, 189
Kenzans 14, 15, 85
King's spear (*Asphodelene lutea*) *94*, 95
Knapweed (*Centaurea nigra*) 124, *125*
Knotweed, small-headed (*Persicaria microcephala*) 232, *233*
Korean burnet (*Sanguisorba hakusanensis*) 115, 122, *123*

L

Larkspur (*Delphinium consolida* 'Misty Lavender') 184, *185*
Lazy Susans 85
Leach, Bernard 71-72
Lemon 62, *63*
Lemonbalm (*Melissa officinalis*) 102, *103*, 122, *123*
Lenten roses (*Helleborus × hybridus*) 38, *39*
Lichen 37
Lilies (*Lilium*)
    Japanese (*L. speciosum*) 222, *223*
    Martagon (*L. martagon*) 140, *141*
    oriental hybrid (*L. speciosum var. rubrum*) 208, *209*
    Royal (*L. regale*) *134*, 135
    Trumpet (*L. regale*) 142, *143*
Liquorice, Yunnan (*Glycyrrhiza yunnanensis*) 212, *213*
Lloyd, Christopher 113-14, 119
Loosestrife (*Lythrum*) 230, *231*
Love-in-a-mist (*Nigella damascena*) 102, *103*

M

Mabberley, Sue and Ian 217
McCarthy family 157
Mallow, common (*Malva sylvestris*) 27, 102, *103*, 224, *225*, 232, *233*
Maltese cross (*Lychnis chalcedonica*) 140, *141*
maple, coral bark (*Acer palmatum* 'Sango-kaku') 222, *223*
marigolds (*Tagetes*) 135, *176*, 177
    French 180, *181*, 182, *183*
    T. patula 'Bonita' 62, *63*
market gardens 59-60, *61*
marsh mallow (*Althaea officinalis*) 230, *231*
marsh pennywort (*Hydrocotyle vulgaris*) 150, *151*
marshes 149, *154-55*
masterwort (*Astrantia*) 37, 184, *185*, 222, *223*
meadow rue (*Thalictrum*) 122, *123*
    Chinese (*T. delavayi*) 126, *127*, 184, *185*
    lavender mist (*T. rochebrunianum*) 208, *209*
    yellow (*T. flavum* subsp. *glaucum*) 115
meadowsweet (*Filipendula rubra* Venusta') 230, *231*
mental health 203-5, 211
Mexican fleabane (*Erigeron karvinskianus*) 164, *165*
Michaelmas daisies (*Aster × frikartii*) 208, *209*
monkshood (*Aconitum carmichaelii*) 208, *209*
montbretia (*Tritonia disticha*) *228*, 232, *233*
mythology 28

N

Nant-y-Bedd, Brecon Beacons 216, *217*-18
nasturiums (*Tropaeolum*) *138*, 139, 140, *141*, 142, *143*, 180, *181*, 182, *183*
nature, connection with 13, 14, 203-5
New Zealand satin flower (*Libertia ixioides*) 84, *85*
Nicholson, Ben 67
Nicolson, Harold 33-34
ninebark (*Physocarpus* 'Summer Wine') 67, 80, *81*
Norfolk, England 18-20, *21-29*, 144-46, *147-65*

O

oats, golden (*Stipa gigantea*) 212, *213*
Olsen, Helen 192, *194*, 195
ox-eye daisy (*Leucanthemum vulgare*) 124, *125*

P

papyrus 49, 51
parsley (*Petroselinum crispum*) 126, *127*
peas (*Pisum*) 168, *176*, 177, 180, *181*
peony 164, *165*
periwinkle
    Vinca major 82, *83*
    white (*Vinca difformis* 'Snowmound') 82, *83*
Persian buttercup (*Ranunculus*) 80, *81*, 82, *83*
Persian ironwood tree (*Parrotia persica*) 224, *225*
phlox 191
Phlox
    Drummond's (*P. drummondii grandiflora*) 180, *181*
    garden (*P. paniculata*) 164, *165*
photography 8
Plant Library 200-202, *203-13*
plant lifecycle 14-15
plantain lily (*Hosta*) 126, *127*
Plants; Places; People 13-14
pomegranate trees (*Punica granatum*) 60, *61*, 106, *107*
poppies 93
    field poppy (*Papaver rhoeas*) 10, 100, *103*, 108, *109*, 114, 118, *119*, 126, *127*
    ladybird poppy (*Papaver* 'Ladybird') 118, *119*
    opium (*Papaver somniferum*) *138*, 139
    Welsh poppy (*Meconopsis cambrica* var. *aurantiaca*) 162, *163*, 164, *165*
    yellow horned sea poppy (*Glaucium flavum*) 26, *27*
porcelain berry vine (*Ampelopsis glandulosa*) 36, *37*
pottery 71-72, 139, 151

Prairie mallow (*Sidalcea candida* 'Little Princess') 140
prairie mallow (*Sidalcea candida*) *141*
pressing flowers 103
primrose (*Primula vulgaris*) 38, *76, 77,* 230, *231*
prince's feather (*Polygonum orientale*) 198, *199*
Provence, France 96-98, *99-108*
purple fountain grass (*Pennisetum rubrum*) 198, *199*
Pyrus Bontanicals *174-76,* 177

Q
Queen Anne's lace (*Ammi majus*) 126, *127*
queen's wreath (*Protrea volubilis* 'Albiflora') *56,* 57

R
Rainier, Priaulx 77
raspberry foliage (*Rubus idaeus*) 176, *177,* 182, *183,* 184, *185*
red orache (*Atriplex hortensis* 'Red Plume') *188,* 198, *199*
red valerian (*Centranthus ruber*) 27, 28, *29,* 152, *153,* 158
reeds (*Phragmites*)
    Norfolk reed (*P. australis*) 20, 27, 28, *29*
    variegated common (*P. australis variegata*) *230,* 231
Revoil, William and Prune 99
Ribwort plantain (*Platego laceolata*) 108, *109*
rock rose (*Helianthemum*) 94, *95,* 108, *109*
rosemallow (*Lavatera trimestris* Loveliness') *134,* 135, 142, *143*
roses
    Flowers *92, 93, 94, 95,* 152, *153, 158,* 164, *165,* 170, 176, *177, 179-80,* 181, 184, *185,* 190, *222,* 223
    Rosehips *36,* 37, *42,* 43
Rungstedlund, Denmark *186-88, 189-99*
Rushes (*Juncus*) 108, *109,* 150, *151*

S
Sackville-West, Vita 33-34
Salvia 49, 51, *224,* 225
    Blood sage (*S. coccinea*) *56,* 57

S. pratens 'Giant Form' *208,* 209
Sabra spike sage (*S. confertiflora*) *226,* 227, *232,* 233
Sage (*S. greggii*) *164,* 165, 232, *233*
Sandpaper vine (*Petrea volubilis*) *50,* 51
Scabious
    Field scabious (*Knautia arvensis*) *102,* 103, 108, *109,* 140, *141,* 142, *143*
    'Sternkugel' (*Scabiosa stellata*) *106,* 107
Schroeder, Erling 190
Scilla 38
Scott-Smith, Troy 33
Sculpture 67-68, 71
Sea buckthorn (*Hippophae rhamnoides*) 162, *163*
Sea kale (*Crambe maritima*) *37,* 160, *161*
Sea lavender (*Limonium vulgare*) *148, 149,* 150, *151*
Sea rush (*Juncus maritimus*) 150, *151*
Sea thrift (*Armeria maritima*) 148, *149*
Seasons 8, 21
Serge Hill, Hertfordshire, England 200-202, *203-13*
Shand, Christina 225, 226, 232
Shell Museum, Glandford, Norfolk *144-46,* 152, *153*
shrubby sea blite (*Suaeda vera*) 150, *151*
Sicilian honey garlic (*Nectaroscordum siculum*) *94,* 95
Sissinghurst Castle Garden, Kent, England *6,* 30-32, *33-43*
slenderleaf rattlepod (*Crotalaria ochroleuca*) *58*
smoke bush (*Cotinus coggygria*) 184, *185*
snapdragon (*Antirrhinum majus* 'Potomac Lavender', 'Monarch', 'Potomac Dark Orange') *114, 126, 127,* 140, *141, 180, 181, 191, 192*
society garlic (*Tulbaghia violacea*) *60,* 61
Solomon's seal (*Polygantum × hybridum*) *222,* 223

sorrel (*Rumex*) 160, *161*
    red (*R. acetosella*) *126,* 127
Spanish bluebell (*Hyacinthoides hispanica*) *73, 76, 77,* 82, *83*
spindle (*Euonymus europaeus*) *222,* 223
spiny starwort (*Pallensis spinosa*) 108, *109*
Spirea
    bridal wreath (*S. × vanhouttei*) 67, *80, 81*
    Japanese spirea (*S. japonica*) 71, *84,* 85
spontaneity 13
Spry, Constance 161, 199
spurge (*Euphorbia × pseudovirgata*) 118, *119*
St Ives, Cornwall, England *64-66,* 67-85
St John's wort (*Hypericum* 'Magical Universe') 180, *181,* 184, *185*
starflowers (*Ipheion uniflorum*) 38
strawberries (*Fragaria*) *164,* 165
Stuart-Smith, Tom and Sue 203
summer snowflake (*Leucojum aestivum*) *80, 81, 82, 83*
supports 14, *15*
sweet pea (*Lathyrus*) *138,* 139, 140, *141,* 142, *143*
sweet William catchfly (*Silene armeria*) 122, *123*

T
Les Terres de Pierre, Provence, France 96-98, *99-108*
Thunberg's bushclover (*Lespedeza thunbergii*) *210,* 211
toad lily (*Tricyrtis formosana*) *208,* 209
tobacco flower (*Nicotiana* 'Whisper') 122, *123*
tomatoes *180, 181,* 182, *183,* 184, *185*
tools 15, 85
tree mallow (*Malva × clementii* 'Rosea') 122, *123*
Trewyn Studio 67-68, *74-76,* 77
Tulips (*Tulipa*) 71, *80, 81, 82, 83*
Turn End, Haddenham, England *86-88, 89-95*

U
Umbrella milkwort (*Tolpis barbata*) 122, *123*

V
Vases, choosing 85
Vegetables 59-60, *61*
Viola 176, *177,* 208, *209*

W
Wales *214-16,* 217-33
Wall rocket (*Diplotaxis tenuifolia*) 108, *109*
Wand loosestrife (*Lythrum virgatum* 'Dropmore Purple') *126,* 127
Water dropwort (*Oenanthe pimpinelloides*) 124, *125*
Water figwort (*Scrophularia auriculata*) *224,* 225
Weeds 14, 157
Welsh poppy (*Meconopsis cambrica var. aurantiaca*) 162, *163, 164,* 165
Wild carrot (*Daucus carota*) 160, *161,* 184, *185*
Windflower (*Anemone coronaria* 'The Bride') 82, *83*
Wisteria (*Wisteria floribunda* 'Yae-Kokuryū') *222,* 223
Wiveton Hall, Norfolk *156,* 157-65
Woolly bindweed (*Convolvulus languginosus*) *102,* 103, 108, *109*

Y
Yarrow (*Alchillea*) 142, *143*
Yellow bell orchid (*Bauhinia tomentosa*) 48
Yellow horned sea poppy (*Glaucium flavum*) 26, *27*
Yellow loosestrife (*Lysimachia ciliata*) 232, *233*
Yellow rattle (*Rhinanthus minor*) 124, *125*
Yew (*Taxus baccata*) 37

FRONT COVER
'Liquorice, Asters and Oats', p. 213.

BACK COVER
Dyffryn Fernant, p. 229.

ENDPAPERS
The browning bottlebrush flowers of slender-leaved burnet (*Sanguisorba tenuifolia*) dangle above pale lilac asters, p. 204

First published in the United Kingdom in 2026 by Thames & Hudson Ltd, 6–24 Britannia Street, London WC1X 9JD

First published in the United States of America in 2026 by Thames & Hudson Inc., 500 Fifth Avenue, New York, New York 10110

Naturalistic Flowers © 2026 Thames & Hudson Ltd, London

Text and photography © 2026 AESME STUDIO

PAGE 82 Photograph by Paul Laib. © The de Laszlo Collection of Paul Laib Negatives, Witt Library, The Courtauld Institute of Art, London.

PAGE 236 Photograph by Kristin Perers.

All Rights Reserved. No part of this publication may be reproduced or transmitted in any form or by any means, electronic or mechanical, including photocopy, recording or any other information storage and retrieval system, without prior permission in writing from the publisher.

EU Authorized Representative: Interart S.A.R.L.
19 rue Charles Auray, 93500 Pantin, Paris, France
productsafety@thameshudson.co.uk
interart.fr

A CIP catalogue record for this book is available from the British Library

Library of Congress Control Number 2025944581

ISBN 978-0-500-02762-2
01

Printed and bound in China by Toppan Leefung Printing Limited

Be the first to know about our new releases, exclusive content and author events by visiting
thamesandhudson.com
thamesandhudsonusa.com
thamesandhudson.com.au